Modern Thai Food
Martin Boetz

With cocktails
& wine by
Sam Christie

Photography
by
Jeremy
Simons

conran
OCTOPUS

This edition published in 2004 by
Conran Octopus Limited, a part of
the Octopus Publishing Group
2–4 Heron Quays
London E14 4JP

To order please ring Conran Octopus
Direct on 01903 828503

First published in 2003 by
Hardie Grant Books

A catalogue record for this book is
available from the British Library.

ISBN 1 84091 382 7

Photography by Jeremy Simons
Photography assistance by Mark Garrett
Cover and text design by text-art
Typeset by text-art
Printed and bound by Imago
Productions

Longrain Restaurant & Bar
85 Commonwealth Street
Surry Hills 2010
Australia
Tel: 00 61 2 9280 2888
Fax: 00 61 2 9280 2887
www.longrain.com.au

To Longrain staff: past, present & future

Contents

Welcome

Welcome to *Modern Thai Food*.

The recipes in this book are typical of the food that you will find in longrain (pronounced long grain), the name of our restaurant in Surry Hills, Sydney, which opened on 27 August 1999. However, this is a book written for the home kitchen and the home cook.

German boy, Asian food . . . it's not an association that springs readily to mind, and a testament to Australia's diversity that chilli and fish sauce happen to do it for me more than olive oil and balsamic vinegar. Thai food is the food I most enjoy eating and creating. I love the flavours, and working to bring out the best combinations. For me, the smells of Thai basil, kaffir lime leaves and chilli just call to be mixed into a stir-fry of duck and chilli jam — I can imagine the finished dish even as I put the basil into the bag at the market. Other people play golf or paint; balancing flavours is my creative pursuit. I've been cooking Asian food for over ten years now, and I hope to keep doing it for a while more — there's still so much left to learn about the flavour combinations, ingredients and cooking techniques.

My love affair with Thai food began at Darley Street Thai in Sydney's Kings Cross. I was totally blown away by the restaurant and the range of amazing flavours in the food. The first time I went there with Katrina, a friend and fellow chef, we sat in the front room and started with mandarin segments filled with caramelised pork, prawn and peanuts. I then had my first ever betel leaf with prawn, pomelo and roasted coconut, and tasted my first real Thai green curry. It was a taste experience that I'll never forget. We were oohing and aahhing so much throughout the meal and dissecting the flavours that we drew the attention of the waiter, Martin, who asked if we would like to meet the chef. We said yes, and out of the kitchen came David Thompson, charming and so full of information. When he walked away from the table, I knew Darley Street was where I wanted to work.

Little did I know that the same charming man would go on to make me cry and laugh so much — not to mention what I then saw as 'torture' as he booted me into (necessary) shape and the direction that led me to become the cook I am today. Other such charming 'torturers' include David King, Michael

Voumard and Ross Lusted, to name a few. Thank you – you'll all be pleased to know I've joined the best of the 'torturers' myself!

My Longrain day

My Longrain day always starts off with a trip to China or Thaina Town, as the local Thais call it. This is a small strip of specialty Thai produce shops in Camp-bell Street, near Sydney's Chinatown. The smells, the people and the friend-liness can be very chaotic first thing in the morning, but I've come to love this part of my Longrain day, especially when there are new Thai vegetables or fruit around to get me thinking about new dishes.

This part of the day also gives me a chance to touch and smell the fruit and veg, and ensures that Longrain uses the freshest range of hand-selected ingredients.

The recipes in this book are some of my favourite dishes, and a fair few of them have featured on the Longrain menu. I want to stress to all of you who attempt the recipes from this book that much of the success of each recipe relies on tasting throughout the cooking process. The art of 'tasting' was never emphasised to me as a young apprentice, but I can't stress enough how important it is to taste how a dish evolves from being something quite bland to something quite amazing with the addition of fish sauce, lime juice or sugar. Tasting as you go, more than quantities and methods, is the big secret to the success of the finished dish. The strength of some herbs and spices also changes with the seasons and the water levels, so something like coriander leaves may taste stronger in, say, December than in June.

I am terrible when it comes to writing things down after or during the making of a dish – as a result, many of my best dishes have never been the same again – mainly because I've forgotten that little pinch or splash of whatever I had in front of me at the time. So sitting still with pen and paper and a computer and writing the recipes for this book has been quite a challenge.

Cooking Asian food may be a new experience for many people, but relax and enjoy the experience. As with other forms of cooking, there are always opportunities to fix things that go wrong. For example, when something is too hot, add some sugar. When something is too sour, add some salt, sugar and chilli. If something is too salty you can either rescue it by adding some lime juice or . . . throw it out and start again.

Remember when you are preparing Thai food that it is more than likely going to be eaten with rice; the dish has to be well seasoned so that it works when eaten and enjoyed as a dish in its own right and when mixed through rice. There is nothing worse than mixing a dish through rice and finding that the flavours are totally lost. Season generously.

I have no secrets. What I know, I've passed on to you in this book, including all the hints and tips that come from years of hard work in the kitchen.

... of last sauce (and ... Shanghai noodle, perhaps in soy ... and, if you think you'd need a bit more ... more tasty, base and texture on the fire) ... some hot mixture of chilli and sugar? ... fresh bean shoots, and rice juice ...

... now, my whole trick is a mixture of ... finely diced cucumber, ginger, coriander ... and shallots with sweet vinegar. I ... could eat spoonfuls of it on its own. It ... is a great accompaniment to a delicious ... yellow curry (just spoon it on top and ... mix it through the rice and curry) and ... with papers (see page 82).

... I hope the recipes in this book will ... help you become more familiar with Thai ... food. Most make use of ingredients that ... are readily available from Chinese and ... Thai grocers, good greengrocers and ... supermarkets. The basics chapter (from ... page 140) offers recipes for curry pastes ... and dressings, and methods for making ... flavourings such as fresh tamarind, ... crisp-fried shallots and garlic. We've also ... included a glossary to explain some of ... the less usual ingredients and how to ... use them.

... Sam Christie has included some ... food-and-wine matching tips. The strong ... flavours in Thai cookery can play ... merry havoc with some wine, but we ... hope the hints will help you ...

Cocktails

Longrain Cocktails

At what moment does a craze start? At the pull of a cork, perhaps, or at the beat-boom of my one-button mp3 adventure? And what is a moment? A moment really never exists, but something comes along to make us say...

When Longrain manager Justin Balmer walked into the bar one day, he thought, 'Hmm, might make a good cocktail, this,' and set the wheels in motion. At that moment the humble muddled cocktail had arrived, and our way to mix a drink to wow, must have one of those.

Muddling is the essential technique in making the drinks on our luscious cocktail list, the big city cousin of the fabulous drinks of old. The Caipiroska is a Longrain bestseller, while the Brazilian Caipirinha is a drink revival.

The basic method for most of the cocktails is this: roughly cut up your limes, put them in a short sturdy glass. Add raw sugar and a little liquid to taste. Then, and muddle those limes until their juices flow. Crush ice, top it off with more ice, cover with a metal shaker and make like you're in a rhythm section of a brass band. Upend back into the glass.

One of the simple philosophies of the Asian kitchen is balance. When you're using plenty of fish sauce and lime juice, you need to add a little palm sugar to even things up. And so it is with Longrain cocktails – fresh, seasonal ingredients and uncomplicated recipes.

We offer new takes on old classics, for instance the 'Rose Porteous', a cheekily rejigged version of the classic 'Suzie Wong'. Or Longrain's emphatically Asian take on the Bloody Mary – vodka, lemon, nahm jim (a Thai sauce of chilli and lime), coriander root and green chilli, with tomato juice, garnished with a sliver of cucumber.

And, if bending the rules appeals, how about a flavoured Martini, using apple, lychee or for the truly adventurous, a Green Fairy, made with absinthe, lemon grass vodka and lemon juice. Here's to love, truth and beauty, the Longrain way.

There are more than 50 cocktails on the Longrain list - including five 'Virgin' drinks - and not counting the nine vodka/gin variations offered on the standard Martini. Why have a standard 'dry white' when you can tuck into a Ping Pong, Citrus Bitch or the new kid on the block, a My Thai, made with no fewer than three infused vodkas, lemon juice and mint?

Bartenders at Longrain are chosen for their dedication, attention to detail and creativity. Guys like Jules, Derrek, Martin, Rico, Sanchez and Jeremy have infused not just the house vodkas but the complete bar with their enthusiasm, deft touch and professionalism. Their influence at the beginning is still evident today in every drink made at the Longrain bar.

More than just marking time in a waiting room for the main event, enjoying a few drinks in the Longrain lounge-bar is an integral part of the dining experience. Peckish patrons can share a bar platter of nahm jim oysters, smoked trout on betel leaves, Thai fish cakes or grilled cuttlefish while relaxing over a cocktail or three.

At Longrain, the living is easy.

Sam Christie

Bar Equipment

COCKTAIL SHAKER ...the Boston shaker is made of a stainless steel tin and a separate glass...

MEASURE/JIGGER ...everything is measured in millilitres (ml). A standard shot is 50 ml (2 fl oz), which is also the size of your standard shot glass.

GLASSWARE When making the longdrink cocktails in this book, you'll need three basic types of glassware:

- a tall glass (highball/collins glass)
- a short glass (tumbler/old-fashioned/short glass)
- a cocktail...

Techniques

Muddling

When muddling drinks a variety of kitchen tools can be used, but generally a wooden pestle or the end of your everyday rolling pin can be used to 'muddle', that is, to crush or bruise fruit, sugar and herbs. Muddling helps to macerate and break down fruit pulp, and with fruit such as limes, muddling with their skins on helps to release the oils and flavours that are contained in the skin.

Other equipment you'll need for muddling include a chopping board, sharp knife, ice cubes (the smaller the better), caster (superfine) sugar and Sugar Syrup (see page 159).

Infusing

Spirits such as vodka, gin, tequila and vermouth can be flavoured with spices, herbs, fresh fruit, chillies, chocolate, even gold leaf. Let the alcohol steep with the ingredients for a few days until the alcohol takes on the 'essence' or flavour of the infusion ingredient.

Begin with good quality spirit such as vodka. Start off with small batches so you don't waste the vodka while experimenting. Fresh ingredients are best, but tinned fruit such as lychee can be used. A little sugar can sweeten the flavour.

Put your ingredients into a clean, dry, airtight jar or container (reserve the vodka bottle for later use). Leave in a warm place (not directly in sunlight, but at room temperature) for 2-7 days. Shake the mixture several times during this period.

The great thing about infusions is that you can see and smell when it is ready and when it isn't. Taste until it reaches the desired strength. If the final result is too strong, dilute with neat, unflavoured vodka.

Once ready, strain the liquid back into the original (or spare) vodka bottle. The infusion will produce a coloured, flavoured vodka ready for use.

Store the infused vodka in the fridge or freezer. Large bottles of vodka look great with the infusion ingredients in them. However, it is important that the ingredient be removed once the desired taste is achieved.

The following amounts are for when you are adding ingredients directly to a 700 ml (23 fl oz) bottle of vodka.

- Blueberries: 15. Blueberry-infused vodka is used to make Purple Haze (see page 13).
- Honeycomb: 5 teaspoons fresh honey or use fresh honeycomb that has been cut into small pieces. Honeycomb-infused vodka is used to make the Alinghi (see page 12).
- Lychees: 8 fresh lychees. Used to make the Lychee Martini (see page 12).
- Vanilla bean: 2, sliced down the centre.
- Watermelon: 6 long slices.
- Raspberries or strawberries: 12 raspberries or 6 ripe strawberries, sliced.
- Cinnamon: 2 sticks.
- Cucumber: 1 whole cucumber, peeled and cut into long slices.
- Citrus: lime and lime zest.
- Chilli: 4 whole red chillies (bird's eye).
- Kaffir lime leaf and lemongrass: 3 kaffir lime leaves and 1 stalk bruised lemongrass.
- Coffee: 20 roasted beans.

Bloody Longrain Mix

Makes 1 litre (1³/₄ pt)

4 red bird's eye chillies
4 coriander roots and stems
200 ml (7 fl oz) Red Chilli Nahm Jim
    (see page 150)
800 ml (27 fl oz) tomato juice (bottled
    or canned)

Combine all the ingredients in a blender or food processor and pulse well. Refrigerate and use the mix within 48 hours.

Bloody Longrain

Makes 1

ice
60 ml (2 fl oz) vodka
Bloody Longrain Mix (see recipe above)
1 long slice of cucumber
1 lemon wedge

Half-fill a high-ball with ice. Add the vodka, then top the rest of the glass with the Bloody Longrain Mix. Stir, and garnish with the cucumber and lemon wedge.

Bloody Longrain

Caipiroska

Caipiroska

MAKES 1

1 large lime
1 teaspoon caster (superfine) sugar
ice

60 ml (2 fl oz) vodka
20 ml (⅔ fl oz) Sugar Syrup (see page 159)

Cut the lime into eighths (leave the skin on). Muddle the lime and sugar in a cocktail shaker. Add the ice, vodka and sugar syrup. Shake vigorously and pour into a tumbler.

To make a Caipirinha simply replace the 60 ml (2 fl oz) vodka with 60 ml (2 fl oz) Cachaca (Brazilian cane spirit). White rum or tequila can also be used.

Ping Pong

MAKES 1

4 fresh lychees, peeled and seeded
pulp of 1 ripe passionfruit
1 teaspoon caster (superfine) sugar
ice

juice of 1 lime wedge
15 ml (½ fl oz) Sugar Syrup (see page 159)
50 ml (1¾ fl oz) citron vodka
a dash of lychee liqueur (optional)

Muddle the lychees, passionfruit and sugar in a cocktail shaker. Add the ice, lime wedge, sugar syrup and spirits. Shake vigorously and pour into a tumbler.

Camp Bitch

MAKES 1

half a large lime
half an orange
1 teaspoon caster (superfine) sugar
15 ml (½ fl oz) Sugar Syrup (see page 159)

ice
50 ml (1¾ fl oz) Campari
30 ml (1 fl oz) ruby red grapefruit juice

Cut the fruit into small chunks, leaving the skin on. Muddle the lime, orange, sugar and sugar syrup together in a cocktail shaker. Add the ice, Campari and grapefruit juice. Shake vigorously and pour into a tumbler.

Alinghi

1 kiwifruit, peeled
half a fresh lime
1 teaspoon caster (superfine) sugar
ice

50 ml (1¾ fl oz) honey-infused vodka
20 ml (⅔ fl oz) ginger liqueur or 6 thin
    slices fresh ginger

Muddle the kiwifruit, lime and sugar (and fresh ginger if liqueur is not available) together in a cocktail shaker. Add the ice and spirits. Shake vigorously and pour into a tumbler.

Stickmata

MAKES 1

3 halved fresh strawberries, hulled
6 fresh raspberries
6 fresh blueberries
1 teaspoon caster (superfine) sugar

ice
50 ml (1¾ fl oz) currant vodka (or infused
    berry vodka)
juice of 1 lime wedge

Muddle the strawberries, raspberries, blueberries and sugar in a cocktail shaker. Add the ice, vodka and lime juice. Shake vigorously and pour into a tumbler.

Lychee Martini

MAKES 1

3 fresh lychees, peeled and seeded
15 ml (½ fl oz) Sugar Syrup (see page 159)
ice

60 ml (2 fl oz) lychee-infused vodka
15 ml (½ fl oz) Pimms (optional)
1 peeled lychee (garnish)

Muddle the lychees and sugar syrup in a cocktail shaker. Add the ice and spirits. Shake vigorously and strain into a chilled martini glass. Garnish with the lychee.

Purple Haze

Rose Porteous

Purple Haze

MAKES 1

45 ml (1½ fl oz) blueberry-infused
    vodka
15 ml (½ fl oz) vanilla liqueur
    (optional)
juice of 1 lime wedge
30 ml (1 fl oz) apple juice
15 ml (½ fl oz) fresh lemon juice
dash of Sugar Syrup (see page 159)
ice
5 fresh blueberries (garnish)

Combine all the ingredients in an ice-
filled cocktail shaker. Shake vigorously
and strain into a chilled martini glass.
Garnish with the blueberries.

Rose Porteous

MAKES 1

4–5 small chunks watermelon
7–10 mint leaves
1 teaspoon caster (superfine) sugar
ice
50 ml (1¾ fl oz) citron vodka
15 ml (½ fl oz) watermelon liqueur
    (optional)
a dash of fresh lime juice
a dash of cranberry juice
a dash of Sugar Syrup (see page 159)

Muddle the watermelon and mint with
the sugar in a cocktail shaker. Add a
scoop of ice. Add the spirits, juices and
sugar syrup. Shake vigorously and pour
into a tumbler.

Ginger Martini

MAKES 1

4 small slices fresh ginger
15 ml (½ fl oz) Sugar Syrup (see page 159)
ice

60 ml (2 fl oz) vodka
15 ml (½ fl oz) ginger liqueur (optional)
fresh ginger, julienned (garnish)

Muddle the sliced ginger and sugar syrup in a cocktail shaker. Add the ice and spirits.
Shake vigorously and strain into a chilled martini glass. Garnish with the julienned ginger.

My Thai

MAKES 1

4 thin slices ginger
8 mint leaves
15 ml (½ fl oz) Sugar Syrup (see page 159)
ice
30 ml (1 fl oz) cucumber-infused vodka

30 ml (1 fl oz) kaffir lime and lemongrass-
    infused vodka
20 ml (⅔ fl oz) chilli-infused vodka
1 whole red chilli (garnish)

Muddle the ginger, mint and sugar syrup in a cocktail shaker. Add the ice and spirits.
Shake vigorously and strain into a chilled martini glass. Garnish by floating the chilli in the drink.
Do not eat the garnish!

Starters

Betel Leaves with Smoked Trout, Galangal & Trout Roe

THE SMOKINESS OF THE SMOKED TROUT IN THIS DISH IS CUT WITH FRESH LIME JUICE – THE SWEET AND SOUR FLAVOURS ARE VERY LIGHT AND HERBACEOUS.

MAKES 20

80 ml (2³/₄ fl oz) Red Chilli Nahm Jim (see
    page 150)
400 g (14 oz) smoked river trout, flesh
    flaked and skin off
2 red shallots, peeled and thinly sliced
2 long red chillies, seeded and julienned
3 kaffir lime leaves, julienned
25 g (1 oz) coriander leaves
20 betel leaves
50 g (1³/₄ oz) trout roe
crisp-fried shallots

Paste
10 cloves garlic, peeled
500 ml (18 fl oz) vegetable oil
6 dried long red chillies, seeded
5 tablespoons dried prawns (shrimp)
1 x 5 cm (2 in) piece galangal, peeled
    and finely sliced
100 g (3½ oz) palm sugar, shaved
100 ml (3½ fl oz) fish sauce

TO MAKE THE PASTE, blend or finely chop the garlic. Heat the oil in a wok and deep-fry the garlic until it is the colour of lightly stained pine. It will keep cooking after it's taken out. Strain and drain the garlic on absorbent paper. Reserve the oil.

Return the oil to the wok and heat. Add the chillies and move them around in the oil until they change colour to a deep red, 10–12 seconds. Remove and drain.

Soak the dried prawns in warm water for 10–20 minutes until soft. Drain.

Dry-roast the galangal in a pan until fragrant. Set aside to cool.

Pound the garlic, galangal, dried prawns and chillies to a fine paste in a mortar and pestle or blend in a food processor with 100 ml (3½ fl oz) of the reserved garlic oil to help the blades move.

Remove the paste from the blender. Place in a heavy-based saucepan on a moderate heat to bring all the flavours together. Add the palm sugar and fish sauce, and stir until the paste is amalgamated and fragrant. Do not caramelise the sugar – just allow it to melt into the paste or it will set hard when cooled. Remove from the heat and cool.

To assemble, place 2 tablespoons of cooled paste in a bowl. Add some Red Chilli Nahm Jim and stir to get a thick, sauce-like consistency.

Add the flaked fish, shallots, chillies, lime leaves and coriander and gently bring together to bind all the ingredients. Spoon onto betel leaves, top with the trout roe and crisp-fried shallots. Repeat with the rest of the ingredients.

Oysters with Red Chilli Nahm Jim

Makes 16

16 oysters, freshly shucked
1 quantity Red Chilli Nahm Jim (see
    page 150)

crisp-fried shallots
coriander leaves

Place the shucked oysters on a serving plate and spoon the Red Chilli Nahm Jim over each.
Garnish with crisp-fried shallots and coriander leaves.

Oysters in Coconut Cream with Trout Roe, Basil & Lime

Serves 4

12 Pacific or large oysters, shucked
25 g (1 oz) coriander leaves
15 g (½ oz) Thai basil leaves
1 green chilli, seeded and julienned
flesh of 1 young coconut, julienned
juice of ½ lime
50 g (1¾ oz) trout roe
2 kaffir lime leaves, julienned

Dressing
1 clove garlic, peeled
3 small bird's eye chillies
150 ml (5 fl oz) coconut cream
½ tablespoon caster (superfine) sugar
50 ml (1¾ fl oz) fish sauce

TO MAKE THE DRESSING, pound the garlic and chillies together. Heat the coconut cream to just below boiling point – be careful not to boil or the cream will split. Add the pounded garlic and chilli, sugar and fish sauce. Taste: the flavour should be creamy, salty, hot and slightly sweet.

Add the oysters to the dressing just to warm through, take out and put in a mixing bowl. Add the coriander, basil, chilli and coconut flesh and toss with some of the dressing. Add a little lime juice to freshen the flavours.

Transfer the salad to plates, spoon on some trout roe and sprinkle with lime leaf.

Eggnets with Pork, Prawn, Beansprouts & Cucumber Relish

SERVES 4

4 medium-sized eggs, beaten
vegetable oil
1 quantity Cucumber Relish (see page 158)

Coconut Caramel Sauce
2 cloves garlic, peeled
3 coriander roots, scraped and cleaned
1 x 2.5 cm (1 in) piece ginger, peeled
5 white peppercorns
100 g (3½ oz) palm sugar, shaved
flesh of 1 coconut, finely grated with a zester
1 teaspoon shrimp paste, roasted and ground
2 teaspoons Shrimp Floss (see page 158)
50 ml (1¾ fl oz) fish sauce

50 ml (1¾ fl oz) water
juice of ½ lime

Filling
4 raw tiger prawns (shrimp), peeled, deveined and chopped
100 g (3½ oz) lean pork mince
100 g (3½ oz) beansprouts
2 kaffir lime leaves, finely shredded
1 stalk lemongrass, white part only, finely sliced
15 g (½ oz) coriander leaves
15 g (½ oz) mint leaves
1 red chilli, seeded and finely sliced
3 tablespoons peanuts, roasted and crushed

Strain the eggs, then leave for a few hours to settle. This allows the proteins in the egg to break down so that it streams when you make the eggnet rather than clumping together.

TO MAKE THE EGGNETS, heat some oil in a non-stick pan. Dip your fingertips in the beaten egg and drizzle the mixture over the pan in opposite directions to form a cross-hatch pattern. (This is a messy process, so cover your stove with foil before you start.) Once the egg sets, transfer to a plate. Repeat. You should be able to make 8 eggnets. If making ahead of time, cool and cover with cling film to stop them from drying out.

TO MAKE THE COCONUT CARAMEL SAUCE, pound the garlic, coriander roots, ginger and white peppercorns to a paste in a mortar and pestle. In a heavy-based pot, add as little oil as possible and fry off the paste until light brown. Add more oil if needed (it can be strained off before the sugar is added). Add the palm sugar and stir until it melts (add some hot water if necessary). Let the sugar slightly caramelise, then add the coconut, shrimp paste and floss. Bring the mixture to a light boil, add the fish sauce and water. Stir well and taste – it should be sweet and salty. Set the sauce aside and cool to room temperature.

TO MAKE THE FILLING, toss the prawns in a hot wok in a little oil until just cooked. Remove, and cook the pork. Set aside and cool to room temperature, then mix with the rest of the filling ingredients. Bind the filling with coconut caramel sauce and taste, adjusting if necessary. Add a squeeze of lime for freshness.

To serve, place the eggnet on a serving plate. Put the filling on one side of the eggnet and fold over. Serve individually or as part of a Thai banquet with the Cucumber Relish.

Lon of Pork & Crab

LON IS A SPICY DIP THAT IS GOOD WITH DRINKS. SERVE AS AN APPETISER OR AS PART OF A THAI BANQUET WITH CRISP, RAW VEGETABLES SUCH AS YARD-LONG BEANS CUT INTO 2.5 CM (1 IN) LENGTHS, BABY CORN, CABBAGE, CHICORY, DEEP-FRIED BETEL LEAVES, CRISP FISH CAKE AND CUCUMBER.

SERVES 4

100 ml (3½ fl oz) Chicken Stock (see
   page 65)
50 g (1¾ oz) pork mince
200 ml (7 fl oz) coconut cream
50 ml (1¾ fl oz) tamarind
2½ tablespoons fish sauce
2 teaspoons caster (superfine) sugar
1 red chilli, sliced into rounds

1 red shallot, peeled and finely sliced
1 stalk lemongrass, white part only,
   finely sliced
½ green mango, peeled and flesh julienned
15 g (½ oz) coriander leaves
50 g (1¾ oz) crabmeat
10 mint leaves
juice of ½ lime, to finish

Heat the chicken stock until boiling, add the pork mince and cook, using a spatula to break up any lumps. Now add the coconut cream and tamarind, fish sauce and sugar. Taste for seasoning – it should taste sweet, salty and sour.

Add the rest of the ingredients except the lime juice, fold through and remove the pan from the heat.

Taste, and season with more sugar and fish sauce, making sure the lon has a good depth of flavour as it is to be a dip for raw vegetables.

Place the relish in a serving bowl and stir in the lime juice.

If you like, you can serve the lon with some deep-fried betel leaves. Just dip the leaves in a little tapioca flour and then in the batter recipe on page 90. Fry in hot vegetable oil until golden brown and crisp, about 3 minutes.

Steamed Rice Noodle Rolls with Barbecued Duck & Basil

A SIMPLE LUNCH DISH OR AN ADDITION TO A LARGE DINNER BANQUET. BUY THE DUCK WHOLE FROM CHINATOWN, OR USE THE SOY DUCK RECIPE FROM PAGE 129.

SERVES 4

50 ml (1¾ fl oz) hoisin sauce
1 kg (2 lb) fresh rice noodle sheets, uncut
150 ml (5 fl oz) Yellow Bean Soy Dressing
    (see page 151)
1 barbecued duck, deboned and sliced
100 g (3½ oz) beansprouts
1 bunch Chinese chives

50 g (1¾ oz) Thai basil leaves
1 x 4 cm (1½ in) piece ginger, julienned
200 ml (7 fl oz) Chicken Stock (see
    page 65)
2 red chillies, finely sliced
1 bunch coriander leaves

Unfold the fresh rice noodles and cut along the folds to create large rectangles. Brush the inside of the rectangles with the hoisin sauce, then add the duck, beansprouts, garlic chives, basil and ginger on the bottom third of the sheet. Roll up into tubes and place the rolls in a deep bowl, seam side down. Repeat with the remaining noodle sheets and ingredients.

Bring the stock and yellow bean soy dressing to the boil, then pour over the rolls so they are half covered with stock. The yellow bean dressing will flavour the stock, and form the basis of a delicious sauce.

Place the bowl with the noodles into a steamer that has been set over boiling water, cover and steam for 8 minutes.

Remove the bowl from the steamer and, before serving, garnish with chilli and coriander.

Fish Cakes

Great as an entrée or to serve with drinks. White-fleshed fish that hasn't been frozen is ideal for making fish cakes.

Makes 30

1 kg (2 lb) red fish or whiting fillets, skin off
1 medium-sized egg
½ quantity Red Curry Paste (see page 154)
2½ tablespoons caster (superfine) sugar
2½ tablespoons sea salt

100 ml (3½ fl oz) fish sauce
5 yard-long beans, very finely sliced
15 g (½ oz) Thai basil leaves, finely sliced
5 kaffir lime leaves, finely sliced
vegetable oil

Blend the fish in a food processor until a paste consistency, about 2 minutes. Place in a large stainless steel bowl, add the egg and curry paste and mix thoroughly. Then add sugar, salt and fish sauce.

Add the yard-long beans, basil and lime leaves and mix thoroughly.

Cup your hand, pick up the mixture and slap it into the side of the bowl for 5–10 minutes to get rid of all the air bubbles.

Heat some oil in a pan and fry a small amount of paste to check the seasoning. It should have a salty, sweet, fragrant and hot taste. Once you're satisfied with the flavour, shape the paste into round cakes of about 40 g (1⅓ oz) each and refrigerate for at least 2 hours before frying.

Heat some oil in a wok until just smoking and shallow-fry the fish cakes in batches for 2 minutes on each side until golden brown.

Serve with Sweet Chilli Sauce (see page 151) or Cucumber Relish (see page 158).

Grilled Scallops with Peanut Nahm Jim

GREAT AS A SNACK WITH DRINKS.

SERVES 4

8 scallops on the half-shell, coral still
    attached
vegetable oil
sea salt
1 bunch coriander leaves
1 stalk spring (green) onion (scallion),
    julienned
1 green chilli, seeded and julienned
1 x 2.5 cm (1 in) piece ginger, peeled and
    julienned

Peanut Nahm Jim
50 g (1¾ oz) roasted peanuts
100 g (3½ oz) palm sugar, shaved
50 ml (1¾ fl oz) water
1 clove garlic, peeled
1 green chilli, seeded
1 green bird's eye chilli
1 coriander root, scraped and cleaned
1½ tablespoons chopped ginger
150 ml (5 fl oz) lime juice
50 ml (1¾ fl oz) fish sauce

TO MAKE THE PEANUT NAHM JIM, place the peanuts on a small metal tray or cake tin base.
    Combine the palm sugar and water in a small saucepan and bring to the boil. The water will evaporate, helping the sugar to break down quickly. Let the sugar caramelise slightly, then pour it over the peanuts. Set aside to cool and harden.

    In a mortar and pestle, pound the garlic, chillies, coriander root and ginger to a uniform paste. Pound the peanut toffee into the mix and combine well.

    Pour over the lime juice, mix well and taste: it should be sweet, sour and nutty. Add the fish sauce to balance the flavours – it should now be sweet, sour and salty.

    Brush each scallop with a little oil and season with salt.

    Place the shells under a griller or on top of a grill to heat. Once the shells are hot, cook the scallops for about 30 seconds on each side. Remove the shells and place on a serving plate. Spoon some nahm jim over each scallop.

    Combine the coriander, spring onion, chilli and ginger in a bowl. Dress with the peanut nahm jim and place just enough salad for a mouthful onto each scallop. Serve immediately.

Grilled Scallops with Sweet Pork on Betel Leaves

THE SWEET PORK IS CUT BY THE HOT & SOUR DRESSING, THEN THE SWEETNESS OF THE SCALLOP COMES THROUGH – A GREAT COMBINATION OF FLAVOURS AND TEXTURES.

SERVES 4

vegetable oil
8 large scallops, coral still attached
sea salt
8 betel leaves

Sweet Pork
150 g (5 oz) pork neck
125 ml (4 fl oz) vegetable oil
1 star anise
1 x 1 cm (⅓ in) piece ginger, peeled
1 clove garlic, peeled
1 coriander root, scraped and cleaned
4 white peppercorns
200 g (7 oz) palm sugar, shaved
50 ml (1¾ fl oz) water
50 ml (1¾ fl oz) fish sauce

Hot & Sour Dressing
50 ml (1¾ fl oz) lime juice
½ teaspoon chilli powder
2 tablespoons fish sauce

Salad
½ bunch coriander leaves
½ bunch mint leaves
1 large red chilli, seeded and julienned
1 stalk lemongrass, white part only, finely sliced
2 kaffir lime leaves, finely julienned

TO MAKE THE SWEET PORK, place the pork in a steamer set over a saucepan of simmering water and steam, covered, for 20 minutes or until cooked through. Cool, then cut into 1 cm (½ cm) dice.

Heat 2 cups oil in a wok. Add the pork and shallow-fry over a medium heat until crisp and golden, then drain on absorbent paper.

Place the star anise, ginger, garlic, coriander root and peppercorns in a mortar and pestle and pound to a uniform paste.

Heat 3 tablespoons oil in a pan and fry the paste until fragrant and crisp. Drain away any excess oil. Add the palm sugar and water, and cook over a medium heat until the sugar has caramelised slightly. Add the fish sauce and mix well. Take off the heat and mix in the pork. Set aside until ready to use.

TO MAKE THE HOT & SOUR DRESSING, combine all the ingredients and mix well.

Heat some oil in a non-stick pan. Season the scallops with salt and sear on both sides until golden. Take off the heat and place on the betel leaves. Spoon over the sweet pork, about 1 teaspoon per scallop. Toss the salad ingredients together, moistening with the dressing. Place a little salad on each scallop and serve.

Tea-smoked Oysters with Cucumber & Ginger

THESE OYSTERS MAKE EXCELLENT HORS D'OEUVRES — JUST CUT THE SALAD INGREDIENTS FINELY AND SERVE THE OYSTERS IN THEIR SHELLS WITH THE DRESSING OR IN CHINESE PORCELAIN SPOONS.

SERVES 4

1 quantity Smoking Mix (see page 156)
12 oysters, freshly shucked
½ cucumber, finely sliced lengthwise
1 x 3 cm (1¼ in) piece ginger, peeled and
    julienned
15 g (½ oz) coriander leaves

1 long green chilli, seeded and julienned
80 ml (2¾ fl oz) Sweet Soy & Ginger
    Dressing (see page 152)
juice of 1 lime
crisp-fried shallots

Line a wok with foil. Place the smoking mix ingredients on the foil in the wok. Turn the heat to high and start to smoke the ingredients.

Line a steamer basket with a banana leaf and place the oysters on it.

Place the steamer in the smoking wok, turn off the heat and cover with the steamer lid and let the smoke infuse into the oysters for about 5 minutes. This method gives a caramelised, smoky flavour to the oysters.

Toss all the salad ingredients together, add the oysters and mix well. Spoon over the dressing and squeeze in some lime juice. Put the salad on a serving plate and sprinkle with crisp-fried shallots.

Salads

& Swe...
Ya... Pork ... 45
... Clam ... with
... & Chilli
Cri... ...k & ... Sala...
...awn ... with illi
...alang ... ...sing
Smoked Trout w... ...ana Flower &...

Beef Salad with Thai Aubergine

SERVE THIS SALAD WITH SOME FRESH VEGETABLES ON THE SIDE TO COOL THE MOUTH. THE ROASTED RICE IS A WORTHWHILE ADDITION – IT GIVES THE FINISHED DISH EXTRA TEXTURE AND NUTTINESS.

SERVES 4

1 x 200 g (7 oz) piece beef sirloin
1½ tablespoons thick sweet soy sauce
1½ tablespoons Roasted Rice (see page 156)

Salad
2 small round Thai aubergines, sliced
1 spring (green) onion (scallion), finely sliced
15 g (½ oz) coriander leaves
15 g (½ oz) mint leaves
1 red shallot, peeled and finely sliced
1 red chilli, seeded and julienned

Dressing
100 ml (3½ fl oz) lime juice
1 teaspoon roasted chilli powder
50 ml (1¾ fl oz) fish sauce
3 bird's eye chillies, finely sliced
2½ tablespoons Sweet Chilli Sauce (see page 151)

Rub the soy sauce all over the beef and grill over a medium to high heat until rare, about 8 minutes. Rest for 8–10 minutes.

While the meat is resting, toss all the salad ingredients together.

Slice the beef and mix through the salad, adding the meat juices.

TO MAKE THE DRESSING, combine all the ingredients and mix well. Taste – it should be hot, sour, salty and slightly sweet.

Pour the dressing over the salad and fold through to mix the flavours. Sprinkle over the roasted rice. Serve with some raw, sliced vegetables on the side.

Crisp Salted Pork & Cuttlefish Salad

SERVES 4 AS PART OF A SHARED MEAL

200 g (7 oz) belly pork
50 g (1¾ oz) sea salt
100 ml (3½ fl oz) vinegar
1 litre (2 pt) vegetable oil
150 g (5 oz) cuttlefish or squid, cleaned and
    scored on the underside
4 spring (green) onions (scallions), shredded
2 red chillies, julienned
1 x 4 cm (1½ in) piece ginger, peeled and
    julienned

1 bunch coriander, washed and chopped
1 bunch mint, washed and chopped
3 green bird's eye chillies, finely sliced
1 red shallot, peeled and finely sliced
1 stem Chinese celery, finely sliced
150 ml (5 fl oz) Yellow Bean Soy Dressing
    (see page 151)
juice of 1 lime

Set a steamer over boiling water and steam the pork, covered, for 35 minutes until cooked. Cool slightly, then prick the skin all over with a fork and massage the salt and vinegar into the skin. Rub a little salt and vinegar on the other side as well. Place the pork on a cake rack with a tray underneath to catch any drips as the pork cools. When cool, remove the pork from the rack and refrigerate for 1–2 hours until it firms (this makes the pork easier to slice).

Slice the pork into long, fine strips along the grain.

Heat the oil in a wok until just smoking and fry the pork until brown and crisp, 3–4 minutes. Drain on absorbent paper and set aside.

Bring a pot of water to the boil, add salt to season and blanch the cuttlefish. Once it curls up, it's done. Refresh in cold water and set aside. You can grill the cuttlefish instead of blanching if you like – rub with some thick sweet soy sauce first before grilling.

Mix the rest of the ingredients together in a bowl. Toss the crisp pork and cuttlefish with the salad and place on a serving plate.

Seared Salmon Salad with a Roasted Shallot & Chilli Dressing

ONE OF MY FAVOURITE SALADS — THE DRESSING HAS GREAT DEPTH OF FLAVOUR FROM THE ROASTED SHALLOTS AND FRIED CHILLIES.

SERVES 4 AS PART OF A SHARED MEAL

2½ tablespoons vegetable oil
200 g (7 oz) salmon fillet
1 tablespoon crisp-fried garlic

Dressing
3 long dried chillies, seeded and fried
    until crisp
½ teaspoon sea salt
50 g (1¾ oz) caster (superfine) sugar
2 red shallots, roasted and peeled
100 ml (3½ fl oz) lime juice

Salad
1 spring (green) onion (scallion), sliced
    lengthwise
½ cucumber, sliced lengthwise
1 long red chilli, julienned
2 red shallots, roasted, peeled and halved
½ bunch coriander leaves
½ bunch mint leaves

TO MAKE THE DRESSING, pound the chillies with the salt and sugar in a mortar and pestle until almost a powder. Add the shallots and pound until a uniform paste. Add the lime juice and mix well with a spoon. Check the seasoning: it should taste sweet, hot and sour with a good caramel flavour.

Heat the vegetable oil and sear the salmon on both sides in a pan until medium rare, about 1½ minutes on each side. Take off the skin and reserve. Cut the fillet into 6 pieces.

Place the salmon in a mixing bowl and add the salad ingredients. Bind the ingredients together gently with the dressing.

Place the salmon skin in a pan with a little hot oil and fry for 2 minutes. Drain on absorbent paper.

Place the salad onto a serving plate, spoon over a little more dressing, garnish with the crisp salmon skin and fried garlic.

Green Papaya Salad with Coconut Rice

A CLAY MORTAR AND PESTLE IS IDEAL FOR MAKING THIS DISH — THE PESTLE IS MADE OF WOOD, WHICH BRUISES THE INGREDIENTS WITHOUT CRUSHING THEM.

SERVES 4

2 green bird's eye chillies
1 clove garlic, peeled
1½ tablespoons shaved palm sugar
1½ tablespoons dried prawns (shrimp),
    soaked in warm water for 10 minutes
1 ripe tomato
1 yard-long bean, cut into 2.5 cm (1 in) pieces
1½ tablespoons tamarind
1½ tablespoons lime juice

1½ tablespoons fish sauce
5 tablespoons roasted peanuts, crushed
1 medium-sized green papaya, finely
    shredded
½ small round Thai aubergine, sliced

Coconut Rice
200 g (7 oz) jasmine rice
375 ml (13 fl oz) coconut milk

TO MAKE THE COCONUT RICE, wash the rice, cover with coconut milk and cook as you would normal rice.

Add the chillies and garlic to a clay mortar and pestle and pound to a paste. Add the palm sugar and drained dried shrimp, lightly bruise, then add the tomato and snake bean. Pound and bruise; the liquid released will form a light sauce. Add the tamarind, lime juice and fish sauce. Taste — it should be sweet, sour and salty. If you think it's intense, remember that the green papaya is yet to be added. Add the peanuts and mix through.

Add the green papaya and Thai aubergine and pound. With your hand and a spoon, mix to combine all the flavours in the mortar. Taste and adjust the seasoning if necessary. Spoon onto a serving plate and serve with coconut rice.

Shredded Chicken & Wingbean Salad

SERVES 6 AS PART OF A SHARED MEAL

500 ml (18 fl oz) coconut cream
500 ml (18 fl oz) Chicken Stock (see
    page 65)
10 kaffir lime leaves
2 stalks lemongrass, bruised and sliced
1 x 5 cm (2 in) piece galangal, peeled
    and sliced
100 ml (3½ fl oz) fish sauce
100 ml (3½ fl oz) oyster sauce
1½ tablespoons caster (superfine) sugar
2 chicken breasts, skin on
crisp-fried shallots
lime wedges

Salad
200 g (7 oz) wingbeans
2 red chillies, seeded and julienned

100 g (3½ oz) coconut flesh, shredded
    using a zester
2 red shallots, peeled and finely sliced
3 kaffir lime leaves, finely shredded
1 stalk lemongrass, white part only,
    finely sliced
15 g (½ oz) mint leaves
15 g (½ oz) coriander leaves
15 g (½ oz) Thai basil leaves

Dressing
100 ml (3½ fl oz) coconut cream
1 clove garlic, peeled
3 green bird's eye chillies
50 ml (1¾ fl oz) fish sauce
1 teaspoon caster (superfine) sugar
juice of ½ lime

Pour the coconut cream and stock into a large, deep pot. Bring to the boil and add the lime leaves, lemongrass, galangal, fish and oyster sauces and sugar and infuse for 5 minutes.

Wash and drain the chicken, add to the simmering coconut broth and poach for 25–30 minutes over a low heat. When ready, remove the chicken and drain the breast on a plate or cake rack. Strain the broth and reserve for use as a delicious soup base. You will need 100 ml (3½ fl oz) broth for the dressing.

Shred the chicken meat with your fingers, tearing along the grain to get long thin strips.

TO MAKE THE SALAD, steam or blanch the wingbeans. Cut them into bite-sized pieces and toss with the other salad ingredients.

TO MAKE THE DRESSING, combine the reserved broth with the coconut cream in a saucepan and heat.

Pound the garlic and chillies to a paste. Add to the hot liquid, season with fish sauce and sugar. Do not boil – keep the mixture on a gentle simmer.

Add the chicken to the dressing and warm through, then pour over the salad. Toss and serve immediately. Garnish with some crisp-fried shallots and lime wedges.

Crisp Noodle Salad with Chicken

I USE WAISEN RICE VERMICELLI FOR THIS DISH, WHICH IS A REINTERPRETATION OF THE FAMOUS MEE GROB.
YOU CAN GARNISH WITH FINELY SHREDDED OMELETTE AND A WEDGE OF LIME.

SERVES 4

2½ tablespoons vegetable oil
200 g (7 oz) chicken mince
5 raw tiger prawns (shrimp), shelled,
    deveined and chopped
150 g (5 oz) palm sugar, shaved
100 g (3½ oz) yellow beans, mashed to
    a paste
4 tablespoons fish sauce
juice of 1 mandarin

Noodles
100 g (3½ oz) rice vermicelli
1 egg, for eggwash
vegetable oil for deep-frying

Salad
4 stalks garlic chives, cut into 1 cm (⅓ in)
    lengths
1 red chilli, julienned
zest of ½ mandarin, julienned
1 red shallot, peeled and finely sliced
1 head pickled garlic, finely sliced
2 squares hard bean curd, diced and
    deep-fried
15 g (½ oz) coriander leaves

Soak the noodles in water (from the tap will do) for 20 minutes until soft. Drain and spread out on absorbent paper to absorb any excess moisture. Separate the noodles into individual strands as much as possible. Lightly brush the noodles with a little eggwash – this will make the noodles turn a golden colour when cooked.

Heat the vegetable oil in a wok until just smoking. Pick up small bunches of noodles at a time, and drop them into the hot oil in batches. They should separate and cover the surface of the oil and look like a spider's web. When it finishes sizzling (about 30 seconds), remove the noodles with a Chinese spider (spatula). Drain on absorbent paper. Repeat with the remaining noodles.

Heat the oil in a wok and stir-fry the chicken and prawns until cooked. Drain away any excess liquid and set aside.

In a heavy-based pan, melt the palm sugar with a little water to help break down the sugar. Allow the sugar to caramelise, then add the yellow beans and fish sauce and combine until thickened. Remove from the heat and fold through the chicken and prawn mixture. Set aside.

When ready to serve, place the chicken in a mixing bowl and add the mandarin juice. Mix well. Toss in all the salad ingredients and lightly mix to bind all the ingredients together. Break up the crisp noodles and toss through the salad. Serve at once, as the noodles lose their crispness if left to sit for too long.

Grilled Cuttlefish & Pomelo Salad

THE CARAMELISED SWEETNESS OF CUTTLEFISH OR SQUID IS A NICE FOIL FOR THE FRESH HERBS AND CHILLIES. YOU CAN ADD A QUARTER OF A BANANA BLOSSOM, FINELY SLICED, TO THIS SALAD, FOR EXTRA TEXTURE.

SERVES 6 AS PART OF A SHARED MEAL

200 g (7 oz) cuttlefish or squid, scored
a splash of thick sweet soy sauce
1 quantity Red Chilli Nahm Jim (see
    page 150)
crisp-fried shallots

Salad
1 pomelo, peeled and segmented
1 stalk lemongrass, white part only,
    finely sliced
2 kaffir lime leaves, julienned
1 bunch coriander leaves
1 bunch mint leaves
1 long red chilli, seeded and julienned
¼ cucumber, shaved into ribbons
1 red shallot, peeled and finely sliced

Toss the cuttlefish with the sweet soy sauce before grilling.

Heat a grill and cook the cuttlefish over a medium to high heat for about 3 minutes.

Place the cuttlefish in a mixing bowl, add the salad ingredients and half the Red Chilli Nahm Jim. Toss the ingredients to mix well.

Place on a serving plate, drizzle over the remaining nahm jim and garnish with some crisp-fried shallots.

Grilled Octopus with Pineapple, Mint & Sweet Chilli

SERVES 4 AS PART OF A SHARED MEAL

50 ml (1¾ fl oz) thick sweet soy sauce
200 g (7 oz) octopus, cleaned and blanched

Dressing
100 ml (3½ fl oz) lime juice
2 tablespoons shrimp floss
½ teaspoon chilli powder
2½ tablespoons Sweet Chilli Sauce (see
    page 151)
2 green bird's eye chillies, sliced

Salad
100 g (3½ oz) cored and peeled pineapple,
    sliced into thin strips
15 g (½ oz) coriander leaves
15 g (½ oz) mint leaves
1 red chilli, seeded and julienned
1 spring (green) onion (scallion), julienned

Rub the thick sweet soy sauce over the octopus. Heat a grill and cook the octopus until the surface is caramelised and a nice golden colour.

TO MAKE THE DRESSING, combine all the ingredients in a bowl and mix well.

Place all the salad ingredients in a bowl, add the warm octopus and moisten with the dressing. Finish with more shrimp floss and some crisp-fried shallots if you like.

Yabby & Pork Salad

SERVES 4

4 yabbies or 4 large raw tiger prawns (jumbo shrimp)
200 ml (7 fl oz) Chicken Stock (see page 65)
200 g (7 oz) lean pork mince
100 ml (3½ fl oz) fish sauce
1 teaspoon caster (superfine) sugar
1 teaspoon roasted chilli powder
15 g (½ oz) coriander leaves

15 g (½ oz) mint leaves
2 red shallots, peeled and sliced
2 spring (green) onions (scallions), cut into small, fine rounds
5 flat-leaf coriander leaves, finely sliced
juice of 2 limes
2 tablespoons Roasted Rice (see page 156)

Steam the yabbies or prawns in a steamer set over boiling water for about 3 minutes until the shells turn red. Remove the tail shell and crack the claws.

In a wok, heat the chicken stock and add the pork. Cook and break up the lumps with the spatula so that the mince is loose. Add fish sauce, sugar and chilli powder. Taste – it should be hot and salty. Add the yabbies. Remove from the heat and transfer the mixture to a stainless steel bowl. Add the herbs, lime juice and a tablespoon of the roasted rice.

Spoon onto serving plates and sprinkle with the remaining roasted rice.

Steamed Clam Salad with Basil & Chilli

THIS DISH CAN BE PRE-PREPARED AND MAKES A PERFECT SNACK. SERVE WITH COLD BEERS ON THE BEACH!

SERVES 4 AS PART OF A SHARED MEAL

1 kg (2 lb) pipis or surf clams (vongole)
1 quantity Green Chilli Nahm Jim (see
    page 150)

Salad
25 g (1 oz) Thai basil leaves
15 g (½ oz) coriander leaves
1 x 5 cm (2 in) knob ginger, peeled and
    julienned
4 kaffir lime leaves, finely shredded
1 stalk lemongrass, white part only, finely
    sliced
2 green chillies, seeded and julienned
1 red chilli, seeded and julienned

Steam the clams over boiling water until the shells open. Cool. Save any excess juices from the shellfish.

Prepare the Green Chilli Nahm Jim according to the instructions on page 150.

Pour the dressing over the clams and let it mix with the shellfish juices. It will dilute a bit so don't worry if you thought the nahm jim was too full flavoured to begin with.

Refrigerate the dish at this point if you are pre-preparing.

To serve, mix in the salad ingredients. Toss together and serve in a deep bowl or plate.

Crisp Duck & Lychee Salad

IF YOU ARE BUYING YOUR DUCK FROM A CHINESE FOODSTORE, ASK FOR A SMALL CONTAINER OF JUICE FOR USE IN THE DRESSING. OR YOU CAN USE SOME MASTER STOCK (SEE PAGE 65). YOU CAN USE CANNED LONGANS OR LYCHEES IN PLACE OF THE FRESH — DRAIN AND RINSE THE FRUIT TO REMOVE THE EXTRA SUGAR.

SERVES 4

1 barbecued duck, deboned and cut into thin
    strips or 1 Soy Duck (see page 129)
toasted sesame seeds

Dressing
100 ml (3½ fl oz) duck juices
50 ml (1¾ fl oz) light yellow bean soy
50 ml (1¾ fl oz) dark soy sauce
2½ tablespoons hoisin sauce
1½ tablespoons caster (superfine) sugar
1½ tablespoons Chinese black vinegar
a drop of sesame oil

Salad
2 spring (green) onions (scallions), julienned
3 shallots, peeled and finely sliced
10 lychees, peeled and seeded
25 g (1 oz) coriander leaves
1 cucumber, julienned
1 x 4 cm (1½ in) piece ginger, peeled
    and julienned

TO MAKE THE DRESSING, whisk all the ingredients together in a bowl and adjust the seasoning to taste. The mix of the two soys creates a rich sweetness and the black vinegar should cut through that sweetness to balance the flavours.

TO MAKE THE SALAD, toss the duck and salad ingredients together with the dressing. Sprinkle with toasted sesame seeds. Serve on its own or with rice.

Grilled Prawn Salad with a Green Chilli & Galangal Dressing

KEEP THE HEADS AND TAILS OF THE PRAWNS ON FOR THIS DISH – REMOVE THE SHELL FROM THE MIDDLE SECTION ONLY.

SERVES 4

8 large raw tiger prawns (shrimp), shelled
    and deveined
a splash of fish sauce
crisp-fried shallots

Dressing
1 clove garlic, peeled
1 small knob galangal, peeled
1 tablespoon crisp-fried shallots
1 long green chilli, seeded
2 green bird's eye chillies
50 g (1¾ oz) palm sugar, shaved
150 ml (5 fl oz) lime juice
50 ml (1¾ fl oz) fish sauce

Salad
15 g (½ oz) coriander leaves
15 g (½ oz) mint leaves
1 long green chilli, seeded and julienned
1 x 2.5 cm (1 in) piece young galangal,
    peeled and julienned
2 kaffir lime leaves, julienned
1 stalk lemongrass, white part only,
    finely sliced

Season the prawns with a splash of fish sauce. Heat a grill and cook the prawns until they change colour and are cooked through. You can also pan-fry the prawns. Set aside and reserve any cooking juices.

TO MAKE THE DRESSING, pound the garlic, galangal, shallots and chillies to a uniform paste. Pound in the palm sugar, then add the lime juice and fish sauce. Taste – the dressing should be hot, sweet, salty and sour, with the nuttines of the shallots coming through. Set aside.

Combine the prawns and salad ingredients and spoon over the dressing. Place on a serving plate and sprinkle with more crisp-fried shallots.

Smoked Trout with Banana Flower & Sweet Fish Sauce

WE USE COLD-SMOKED TROUT FILLET FOR THIS DISH. THERE IS NO USE MAKING SMALL QUANTITIES OF THIS DRESSING – IT KEEPS WELL UNREFRIGERATED, AND LENDS ITSELF TO MANY USES, FOR EXAMPLE, OVER GRILLED CHICKEN OR FISH.

SERVES 4

vegetable oil
1 x 200 g (7 oz) fillet smoked sea trout
crisp-fried shallots
lime wedges
crisp-fried garlic

Salad
¼ banana blossom, finely sliced
2 kaffir lime leaves, julienned
10 Thai basil leaves
10 g (¼ oz) coriander leaves
1 red chilli, julienned
2 long, dried red chillies, seeded and roasted

Sweet Fish Sauce
1 x 500 g (1 lb) disc palm sugar, crushed
1 stalk lemongrass, bruised along its length
½ medium-sized red onion, sliced
4 kaffir lime leaves
1 x 2.5 cm (1 in) piece galangal, sliced
4 coriander roots, scraped and cleaned
100 ml (3½ fl oz) tamarind
100 ml (3½ fl oz) fish sauce

Heat some vegetable oil in a pan and shallow-fry the fish on both sides until crisp. Drain on absorbent paper.

TO MAKE THE SWEET FISH SAUCE, melt the palm sugar in a heavy-based pot over a medium heat. Add a little water to help break down the sugar. Once the sugar has melted, add the lemongrass, onion, lime leaves, galangal and coriander roots and bring to the boil. Let the sugar lightly caramelise. The ingredients will release some water into the mixture, so keep reducing until the sugar thickens again. Reduce the heat, add the tamarind and fish sauce, taking care as the mixture will spit. Mix in well and strain, then set aside to cool. The mixture should have a honey-like consistency and taste sweet and salty. If it solidifies, return the mixture to the heat and add a little more fish sauce and tamarind and allow to soften again.

Toss all the salad ingredients together. Cut or break up the fish and stir through. Toss, drizzling more sauce over the salad to coat.

Place on a plate, garnish with the crisp-fried shallots, lime wedges and garlic.

Smoked Fish Salad

The banana leaf should be large enough for the fish to sit on, but not cover all the steamer holes. Sea bass or snapper work well in this dish.

Serves 4 as part of a shared meal

1 quantity Smoking Mix (see page 156)
1 x 10 cm (4 in) square piece banana leaf
1 x 200 g (7 oz) fillet sea bass or snapper
roasted peanuts
lime wedges

Salad
½ cucumber, halved and shaved
6 cherry tomatoes, halved
1 spring (green) onion (scallion), julienned
1 large red chilli, seeded and julienned
15 g (½ oz) coriander leaves
10 g (¼ oz) mint leaves
2 tablespoons roasted peanuts, crushed

Dressing
100 ml (3½ fl oz) sweet vinegar
2½ tablespoons black vinegar
1½ tablespoons thick sweet soy sauce
50 ml (1¾ fl oz) lime juice
4 green bird's eye chillies, finely sliced
¼ teaspoon roasted chilli powder

Line a wok with foil. Place the Smoking Mix ingredients on the foil in the wok. Turn the heat to high and start to smoke the ingredients.

Line a steamer basket with a banana leaf and place the fish on it.

Place the steamer in the smoking wok, turn off the heat and cover with the steamer lid. Let the smoke infuse into the fish for about 5 minutes. This method gives the fish a caramelised, smoky flavour and does not actually cook it.

TO MAKE THE SALAD, toss all the ingredients together in a bowl and set aside.

TO MAKE THE DRESSING, combine all the ingredients in a bowl and whisk together. The dressing should be sharp tasting, with the sharpness being mellowed by the sweet soy and black vinegar.

TO COOK THE FISH, either steam or pan-sear it. Both methods will take about 5 minutes.

Leave the fish fillet to rest for 2–3 minutes, then break up the fish into the salad. Add the dressing, toss and transfer to a serving plate. Place some extra peanuts on top and serve with lime wedges on the side.

Silken Tofu with Pickled Ginger, Cucumber & Mint

A 2.5 CM (1 IN) PIECE OF GINGER, JULIENNED, ALSO WORKS IN PLACE OF THE PICKLED GINGER.

SERVES 4

1 x 200 g (7 oz) packet silken tofu, sliced
100 ml (3½ fl oz) Sweet Soy & Ginger
    Dressing (see page 152)
juice of 1 lime
crisp-fried shallots

Salad
15 g (½ oz) coriander leaves
15 g (½ oz) mint leaves
1 red chilli, seeded and julienned
½ cucumber, finely shaved into ribbons
2 tablespoons Pickled Ginger (see page 157)
1 spring (green) onion (scallion), finely
    sliced diagonally

Place the sliced tofu on a serving plate.

Mix the salad ingredients, combining well. Place on top of the tofu, and spoon over the dressing and lime juice.

Sprinkle over the crisp-fried shallots.

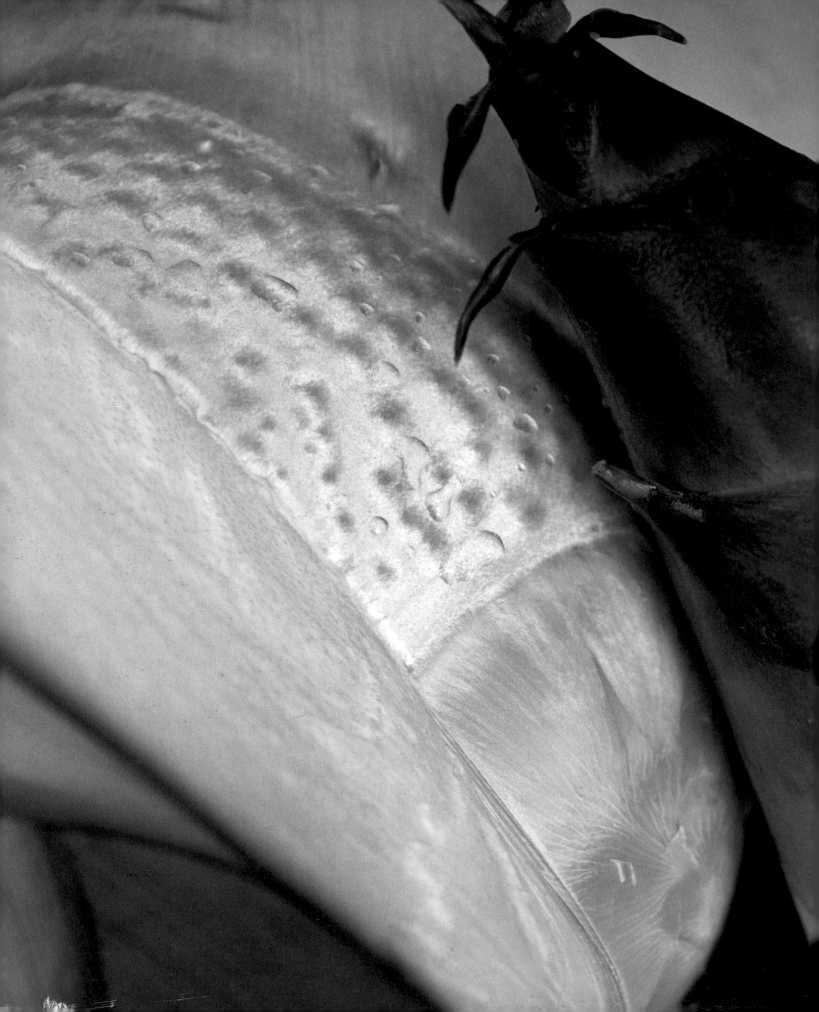

Soups

Hot & Sour Soup of Perch

When the fish is cooked through, the flesh easily lifts off the bone. You can finish cooking the fish in the hot soup stock; as long as you do not boil the soup, the fish will not break up.

Serves 6 as part of a shared meal

750 ml (1 pt 6 fl oz) Chicken Stock (see page 65) or vegetable stock
3 kaffir lime leaves
1 stalk lemongrass, bruised
4 red bird's eye chillies
5 slices galangal
4 tablespoons fish sauce
1½ tablespoons Chilli Jam (see page 150)
2 teaspoons oyster sauce
4 red shallots, peeled and halved
2 coriander roots, scraped and cleaned

6 oyster mushrooms, cut into bite-sized pieces
1 tomato, cut into bite-sized pieces
a splash of fish sauce
1 whole sea perch or 1 x 200 g (7 oz) pack silken tofu
vegetable oil for deep-frying
juice of 1 lime
1 bunch flat-leaf coriander leaves, finely shredded
coriander leaves
Chilli Jam (see page 150)

Bring the stock to a boil in a saucepan and add the lime leaves, lemongrass, chillies, galangal, fish sauce, chilli jam, oyster sauce, shallots and coriander roots. Reduce the heat and simmer for 2–3 minutes to infuse the flavours. Check the seasoning – it should be hot, sour and salty.

Add the mushrooms and tomato. Simmer for another 3 minutes.

Rub fish sauce over the fish.

Heat the vegetable oil in a wok until just smoking and gently lower the fish into the oil. If the fish is fully immersed, fry until golden brown, 6–7 minutes. If the fish is not fully immersed, be sure to turn the fish so that it cooks evenly. Remove and drain on absorbent paper.

In a serving bowl, add the lime juice and flat-leaf coriander. If using tofu, dice and put into the bowl.

Put the fish into the bowl and pour over the hot soup. Garnish with coriander leaves and serve with extra chilli jam on the side.

Chicken Rice Noodle Soup with Chinese Broccoli

IF POSSIBLE, BUY THE NOODLES AS A WHOLE SHEET AND CUT IT WHEN YOU NEED IT. THIS WAY, THE NOODLES WON'T DRY OUT AND YOU CAN HAVE THEM IN YOUR PREFERRED WIDTH.

SERVES 4

300 ml (10 fl oz) Chicken Stock (see page 65)
100 ml (3½ fl oz) Yellow Bean Soy Dressing (see page 151)
1 x 2.5 cm (1 in) piece ginger, peeled and julienned
2 red shallots, peeled and finely sliced
1 chicken breast, sliced into thin strips

2 pieces Chinese broccoli, cut into bite-sized pieces
100 g (3½ oz) fresh uncut Asian rice noodles, cut into 0.5 cm (⅛ in) strips
1 red chilli, finely sliced into rounds
1 bunch coriander leaves
beansprouts
coriander leaves

Place the stock and yellow bean soy dressing in a saucepan and bring to the boil. Lower the heat to a simmer, taste for seasoning and add more yellow bean soy if it tastes too bland.

Add the ginger and shallots. Add the chicken and broccoli and simmer for 3–4 minutes.

In deep soup bowls, place the cut noodles, chilli and coriander and pour over the hot soup. Garnish the soup with beansprouts and more coriander leaves and serve. If you like, squeeze in the juice of ½ lime for extra freshness.

Roasted Duck & Shiitake Mushroom Dumpling Soup

MAKE THIS THE DAY YOU WISH TO SERVE IT. THE BROTH SHOULD BE CLEAN-TASTING, WITH A SLIGHT GINGER AND SPRING ONION FLAVOUR. YOU CAN BUY THE DUCK READY-ROASTED FROM A CHINESE FOODSTORE, OR MAKE YOUR OWN. SHREDDED CHINESE BROCCOLI CAN BE MIXED THROUGH THE SOUP FOR ADDED TEXTURE.

SERVES 4

Dumplings
½ barbecued duck, deboned
6 dried shiitake mushrooms, soaked and
    stems discarded
2 spring (green) onions (scallions),
    finely chopped
1 x 2.5 cm (1 in) piece ginger, peeled
    and julienned
1½ tablespoons hoisin sauce
2 teaspoons oyster sauce
1 packet wonton skins

Broth
500 ml (18 fl oz) Chicken Stock (see page 65)
100 ml (3½ fl oz) light yellow bean soy
2½ tablespoons oyster sauce
½ teaspoon ground white pepper
100 ml (3½ fl oz) thick sweet soy sauce
1 x 2.5 cm (1 in) piece ginger, peeled
    and julienned
2 spring (green) onions (scallions), cut
    into 1 cm (⅓ in) lengths
2 tablespoons crisp-fried garlic

TO MAKE THE DUMPLINGS, mince the duck meat and skin finely. Do the same with the mushroom caps. Toss in the spring onions and ginger and combine. Add the hoisin and oyster sauces and mix well. The mixture should be dryish.

Fill the wonton skins with 1 teaspoon filling per dumpling. Place the filling in the middle of the wonton skin and gather the edges together at the top. Pinch and twist to seal the top. Repeat with the rest of the skins and dumpling mixture. Refrigerate for at least an hour before cooking.

TO MAKE THE BROTH, bring the stock, yellow bean soy, oyster sauce, pepper and sweet soy sauce to the boil in a saucepan. Add the ginger and spring onions. Add the dumplings, and once they float to the top, take the saucepan off the heat.

Ladle the soup and dumplings into serving bowls and garnish with the crisp-fried garlic.

Steamed Duck, Winter Melon & Shiitake Mushroom Soup

FOR BETTER FLAVOUR, MAKE THIS SOUP THE DAY BEFORE IT IS SERVED. LEAVE THE SOUP TO SETTLE SO THAT THE FAT FLOATS TO THE TOP, SOLIDIFIES AND SEALS IN THE SOUP. BEFORE REHEATING, SKIM OFF THE FILM OF SOLIDIFIED FAT.

SERVES 6

4 combined duck leg and thigh, trimmed of
    excess fat
1 small winter melon, peeled and cut into
    bite-sized pieces
1 Thai preserved lime, halved
10 dried shiitake mushrooms, soaked and
    stems discarded
freshly julienned ginger
Chinese chives

Soup
5 cloves garlic, peeled
4 coriander roots, scraped and cleaned
1 x 4 cm (1½ in) piece ginger, peeled
8 white peppercorns
1 small red onion, peeled and sliced
100 ml (3½ fl oz) vegetable oil
100 ml (3½ fl oz) Chinese cooking wine
60 g (2 oz) rock candy, pounded
150 ml (5 fl oz) oyster sauce
100 ml (3½ fl oz) yellow bean soy
1.5 litres (2¾ pt) Chicken Stock (see page 65)

TO MAKE THE SOUP, pound the garlic, coriander roots, ginger, peppercorns and onion in a mortar and pestle until well combined and a uniform paste.

Heat the oil in a heavy-based pot. Add the paste and fry until it smells crisp and nutty. Drain off the excess oil and deglaze the pot with the Chinese cooking wine. Add the rock candy, oyster sauce and yellow bean soy and cover with the chicken stock. Bring to the boil and skim. Strain the stock and keep warm.

Set a large steamer over boiling water. In a bowl that will fit into the steamer, place the duck pieces, winter melon, preserved lime and mushrooms. Place the bowl in the steamer, then pour the strained stock almost to the top of the bowl. Cover with a layer of baking paper, then with foil. Steam the soup for 1½ hours, checking the steamer's water level throughout, refilling with boiling water as necessary.

When done, take the ingredients out of the steamer and check that the duck is cooked through. The meat should fall easily off the bone and the winter melon should be almost translucent. Taste and adjust the seasoning if necessary.

To serve, ladle the soup, duck and winter melon into bowls. Top each with ginger and chives. Serve hot.

Coconut Soup of Prawns & Oyster Mushrooms

THE GOOD OLD FAVOURITE, DTOM KHA GAI, MADE USING THE FRESHEST OF INGREDIENTS. THIS WILL MAKE YOU RESOLVE TO NEVER EAT THE TORTURED VERSIONS AGAIN!

SERVES 4

250 ml (9 fl oz) coconut cream
250 ml (9 fl oz) Chicken Stock (see page 65)
4 kaffir lime leaves
2 stalks lemongrass, bruised along
   the length
1 x 4 cm (1½ in) piece galangal, peeled
   and sliced
4 red shallots, peeled and halved
4 coriander roots, scraped and cleaned
100 ml (3½ fl oz) fish sauce

1½ tablespoons caster (superfine) sugar
50 ml (1¾ fl oz) oyster sauce
2½ tablespoons Chilli Jam (see page 150)
8 raw tiger prawns (shrimp), body shell
   removed and deveined, head and tails
   left on
6 oyster mushrooms
juice of 2 limes
4 green bird's eye chillies, finely sliced
coriander leaves

In a heavy-based saucepan, heat the coconut cream and stock and bring to the boil. Add the lime leaves, lemongrass, galangal, shallots and coriander roots and season with fish sauce, sugar, oyster sauce and chilli jam. Check the seasoning – it should taste hot, salty and sweet, and the flavours of the aromatics should be coming through. Lower the heat to a simmer, add the prawns and mushrooms and cook for a further 4–5 minutes.

Squeeze the lime juice into serving bowls and add the chillies. Pour over the hot soup and garnish with coriander leaves.

Chicken Stock

MAKES 2 LITRES (3½ PT)

3 chicken carcases, all skin and fat removed
2.5 litres (4½ pt) water
4 spring (green) onions (scallions), sliced

1 brown onion, peeled and sliced
2 x 4 cm (1½ in) pieces ginger, sliced

Wash the chicken bones thoroughly to remove any blood. Place in a large stockpot, cover with cold water and bring to the boil. As the water reaches boiling point, scum may float to the surface – skim off with a spoon to ensure a clear stock.

Once boiling point is reached, reduce the heat to a simmer, skim off any more scum and add the aromatics. Simmer for 3–5 hours over a very low heat. Strain.

The stock keeps for 2–3 days, refrigerated. Bring the stock to the boil before using.

Master Stock

MAKES 2 LITRES (3½ PT)

8 cloves garlic, peeled
15 white peppercorns
vegetable oil
125 ml (4 fl oz) Chinese cooking wine
125 ml (4 fl oz) thick sweet soy sauce
250 ml (9 fl oz) oyster sauce

1 stick cassia bark
3 star anise
250 ml (9 fl oz) light yellow bean soy
2 litres (3½ pt) Chicken Stock (see this page)
2 x 4 cm (1½ in) piece ginger, peeled and
    chopped

Pound the garlic and peppercorns to a paste. Fry in a little oil until it smells crisp and nutty. Deglaze with the cooking wine, then add the rest of the ingredients. Bring to the boil, and skim off any scum and excess oil. Simmer for 20 minutes, then strain, discarding all the solids. You can now use the stock to cook your choice of meat or poultry.

Strain the stock after each use and refresh with more ginger and spices each time you use it. I find that the stock can get very strong after several uses, so feel free to start your stock from scratch again.

Longrain

The first time I saw the space that was to be Longrain (I have since sold it, but the kitchen is now located...) The warehouse space was introduced to me by... Sam and Rob Samaie, who were delighted to have finally found a location suitable for a possible restaurant. Sam and Rob wanted me to... design... when... each other, it became clear that I was interested in the whole concept...

My first brief was for a fast, child-friendly restaurant with a jazzy bar and modern Asian food to match. We kept changing and refining the idea until we developed the... that of Longrain that was to serve mostly Thai food...

Since then, many people have come through our doors. We opened on 2... August 2000, which also happened to be my thirtieth birthday. We had to open a week and a half early or about... a week but a new setback would pop up each day. We finally opened the doors for my birthday and had some of my closest friends in our private dining room. So you could say mine was the first birthday celebration there.

The original kitchen team was so on top of things — we had had several practice runs during the weeks before opening — that I was confident enough to leave them to it. Eventually, after too many celebratory and nerve-calming champagnes I sat down to eat and it hit me that it was actually happening — we were officially open!

I was pretty pleased with the food that first night and things have kept evolving — the food has become more complex, we have a terrific bar and the Longrain soundtrack that Sam puts together is fabulous. We're also lucky that many people loved the atmosphere from the first night, and the feel and look of the restaurant.

We ended up seating 75 people that first night. On the second night we fed 105 and I remember quietly saying to Justin after service, 'Darling, I've never cooked for so many people in one service before!'

Those first-night nerves became excitement — it was working!

As a restaurant, we'll keep changing and evolving. Our latest addition is a fishtank. I have always wanted a tank of live seafood at Longrain, something I've noticed in restaurants in Bangkok,

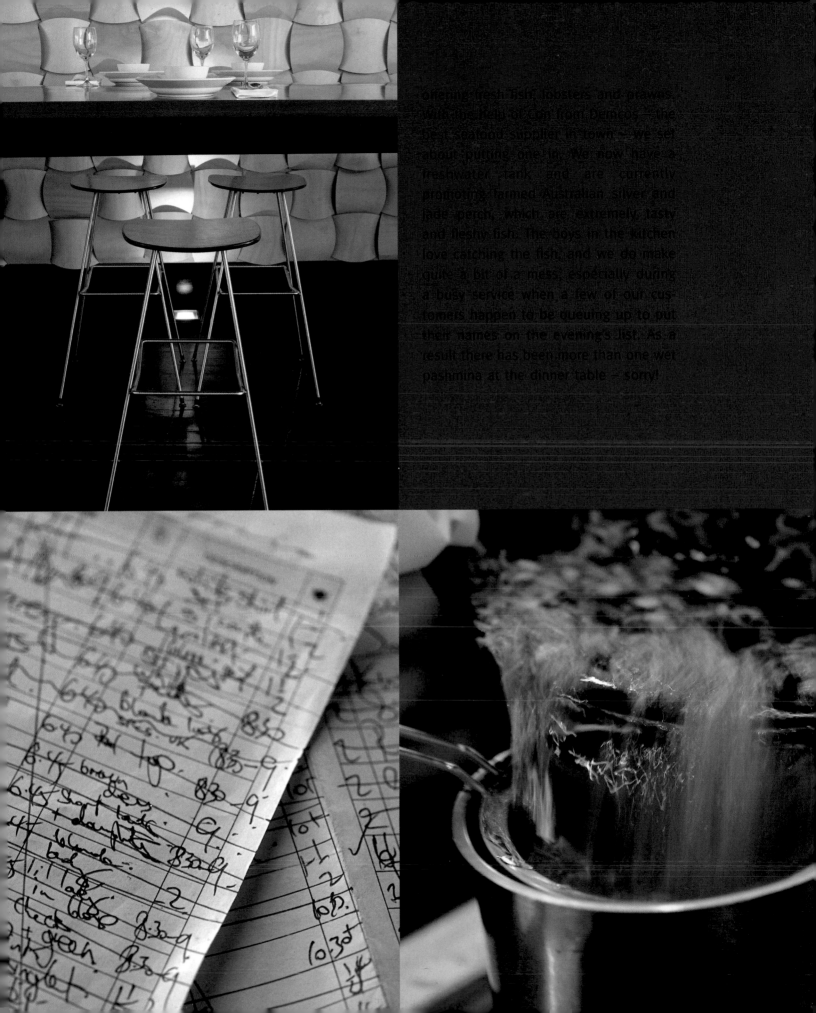

offering fresh fish, lobsters and prawns. With the help of Con from Demcos — the best seafood supplier in town — we set about putting one in. We now have a freshwater tank and are currently promoting farmed Australian silver and jade perch, which are extremely tasty and fleshy fish. The boys in the kitchen love catching the fish, and we do make quite a bit of a mess, especially during a busy service when a few of our customers happen to be queuing up to put their names on the evening's list. As a result there has been more than one wet pashmina at the dinner table — sorry!

Curries

Curry Pastes

The intensity and taste of some ingredients can change with the seasons, so the recipes in this chapter are not strict guides. Go by taste – a batch of coriander, for example, may taste stronger one week and be gentler the next.

Most paste quantities can safely be doubled and frozen. Frozen pastes should be used on the day of thawing for best results.

The easiest way to blend pastes at home is to first pound the ingredients in a mortar and pestle to a uniform paste. Then add them to a food processor or blender. Breaking down the fibres will save the machine from overwork, and pounding them first reduces the need to add extra water to help the blender move as the natural moisture from the ingredients has already been released.

The longer a fresh paste is kept, the more the flavours dissipate, so if possible use within 3 days.

In most dishes, you will have to cook out the curry paste, by which I mean frying the curry paste in coconut cream or vegetable oil until it no longer smells raw – no garlic or onion aromas. The cooked paste should smell nutty, and of caramelised flavours.

When using coconut cream from a tetra pack, dilute with stock.

Coconut Milk

1. Crack the coconut brittle.

2. Set the coconut half over the 'rabbit' grater.

3. Grate the flesh.

4. Grated coconut flesh, put it into the rabbit grater.

5. Add about 250 ml (9 fl oz) hot water to the flesh.

6. Allow the grated flesh to steep in the water for a little while.

7. Place small handfuls of the flesh in a cloth and squeeze firmly.

8. Squeeze the milk into a bowl or ceramic bowl.

9. Allow the coconut milk to settle. The 'coconut cream' will rise to the top; the rest is coconut milk.

Coconut & Chilli Fish Curry with Yard-long Beans

My interpretation of an Indonesian curry, with more aromatics added to give it more flavour. You can poach the fish in the curry mixture if you do not wish to fry it. This curry works well with cod.

Serves 4 as part of a shared meal

100 ml (3½ fl oz) vegetable oil
50 ml (1¾ fl oz) fish sauce
1½ tablespoons caster (superfine) sugar
500 ml (18 fl oz) coconut milk
1 stalk lemongrass, white part only, sliced
4 slices galangal
4–5 kaffir lime leaves
2 red chillies, seeded and halved
3 baby corn, halved
2 yard-long beans, cut into 2.5 cm (1 in) lengths
vegetable oil for deep-frying

200 g (7 oz) cod, sea bass or monkfish fillets
coriander leaves
lime leaves, julienned
50 ml (1¾ fl oz) coconut cream

Chilli Paste
4 red shallots, peeled and sliced
3 long, dried red chillies, soaked
4 kaffir lime leaves

To make the chilli paste, blend all the ingredients together in a food processor until a uniform paste is achieved.

Heat the oil in a wok and fry the paste until fragrant, about 5 minutes, stirring continuously so it doesn't burn.

Add the fish sauce and sugar and stir in. Add the coconut milk and bring to the boil. Add the lemongrass, galangal and lime leaves. Let these infuse at a gentle simmer for about 3 minutes.

Add the chillies, baby corn and yard-long beans.

Meanwhile, heat some oil in a wok until smoking and deep-fry the fish until golden and crisp. Remove and drain.

Break up the fish into bite-sized pieces and place in a serving bowl.

Taste and season the curry mixture with extra fish sauce and sugar if needed. Pour the sauce over the fish, sprinkle with coriander leaves and lime leaves and the extra coconut cream.

Dry Red Fish Curry

If you cannot find pork fat, use vegetable oil instead. The pork fat gives the paste a depth of flavour. Try it with and without and see what you think – pork fat wasn't my choice until I tasted the difference! Any white-fleshed fish would work in place of the sea bass.

Makes 4 individual portions or 2 large shared portions

200 g (7 oz) minced pork back fat
100 ml (3½ fl oz) water
1 teaspoon sea salt
2½ tablespoons Red Curry Paste (see page 154)
1½ tablespoons lesser galangal
3 kaffir lime leaves, torn
1 long red chilli, seeded and sliced
1½ tablespoons shaved palm sugar
50 ml (1¾ fl oz) fish sauce
1½ tablespoons oyster sauce

50 ml (1¾ fl oz) Chicken Stock (see page 65)
200 g (7 oz) sea bass fillet, cut into 50 g (1¾ oz) pieces
1 stick fresh green peppercorns (optional)
2 yard-long beans, cut into 2.5 cm (1 in) lengths
1 small round Thai aubergine, cut into wedges
25 g (1 oz) holy basil leaves
vegetable oil
kaffir lime leaf, julienned

Combine the pork, water and salt in a pan and bring to the boil. As the water evaporates, the pork fat will start to melt. Stir occasionally as the water evaporates. The fat should run clear, with some fat particles starting to look like deep-fried crisp bits. At this stage the pork fat is ready to be strained.

Place a pan on a stove, add the pork fat and heat. Add the curry paste and cook until it smells fragrant, 2–3 minutes. Add the lesser galangal, lime leaves, chilli, palm sugar, fish sauce, oyster sauce and stock. Try not to scorch the paste; if it is too hot, lower the heat and add a little more stock. Check the seasoning for a hot, salty and sweet taste.

Add the fish and peppercorns, if using, and cook for 3–4 minutes, then add the beans, aubergine and half the basil.

Heat some vegetable oil in a wok and fry the remaining basil. Drain on absorbent paper.

Spoon the curry onto a serving dish and garnish with the basil and lime leaf julienne. Serve with rice.

Deep-fried Snapper with Rich Red Curry

GRILLED SHELLFISH SUCH AS CRAYFISH, SCALLOPS OR PRAWNS ARE ALSO DELICIOUS COOKED INTO THIS CURRY.

SERVES 4

150 ml (5 fl oz) fresh coconut cream or
   100 ml (3½ fl oz) vegetable oil
4 tablespoons Red Curry Paste (see
   page 154)
100 ml (3½ fl oz) fish sauce
100 g (3½ oz) palm sugar, shaved
400 ml (14 fl oz) coconut milk
4 kaffir lime leaves
2 long red chillies, seeded and sliced into
   uneven lengths

1 litre (1¾ pt) vegetable oil
1 x 800 g–1 kg (1¾–2 lb) whole snapper,
   cleaned, or 2 x 180 g (6 oz) fillets
   snapper or other white-fleshed fish
   fillets
100 ml (3½ fl oz) fish sauce
15 g (½ oz) Thai basil leaves
red chillies, julienned

Heat a heavy-based pan and add the coconut cream or vegetable oil. If using the coconut cream, keep cooking and stirring until it splits before you add the curry paste. If using the oil, fry the paste until fragrant and the oil is released.

At this point, season with fish sauce and palm sugar, stirring constantly until the sugar has dissolved into the paste.

Moisten with the coconut milk and bring to the boil. Add the lime leaves and chillies and taste for seasoning. Reduce the heat and simmer until thickened, about 5 minutes. Keep simmering on a low heat, stirring from time to time to prevent scorching. Taste and check for seasoning, adjusting as necessary.

Meanwhile, heat the vegetable oil in a wok until just smoking.

Score the whole fish on both sides and douse with fish sauce. If using fillets, rub with fish sauce. Lower the fish into the oil and fry until golden brown. Drain the fish and place on a serving plate.

The curry sauce should now be quite thick, with a small film of oil on the top. Bring it back to a simmer, add the basil, reserving a small handful for garnish.

Spoon the curry sauce over the fish and garnish with the remaining basil leaves and some chilli. A spoonful of coconut cream is also a good garnish, adding richness to the dish.

Peanut Curry of Grilled Beef

SERVES 4

150 ml (5 fl oz) fresh coconut cream or
4 tablespoons Peanut Curry Paste (see
    page 154)
100 g (3½ oz) palm sugar, shaved
100 ml (3½ fl oz) fish sauce
300 ml (10 fl oz) coconut milk
2 long red chillies, seeded and halved

3 kaffir lime leaves, julienned
2 teaspoons roasted peanuts, crushed
200 g (7 oz) rump steak
15 g (½ oz) Thai basil leaves
extra coconut cream

Heat a heavy-based pan and add the coconut cream or vegetable oil. If using the coconut cream, keep cooking and stirring until it splits before you add the curry paste. If using the oil, fry the paste until fragrant and the oil is released.

Add the palm sugar, fish sauce and coconut milk, and bring to the boil. Add the chillies, lime leaves and 1 teaspoon of the peanuts. Simmer until a small film of oil forms on the surface of the mixture. Set aside.

Chargrill or barbecue the beef over a medium to high heat for 5 minutes on each side for medium rare (more if you want the meat more well done), then rest in a warm place for 10 minutes.

Return the curry sauce to a moderate heat and add half the basil.

Slice the beef and place on a serving plate.

Add the beef juices to the curry sauce, then spoon over the beef. Garnish with the remaining peanuts, basil and a splash of coconut cream. Serve with steamed rice.

Pineapple Curry of Grilled Pork

SEAFOOD WORKS WELL IN PLACE OF THE PORK; TRY THE CURRY WITH MUSSELS.

SERVES 4

150 ml (5 fl oz) fresh coconut cream or
 100 ml (3½ fl oz) vegetable oil
4 tablespoons Red Curry Paste (see
 page 154)
100 g (3½ oz) palm sugar, shaved
100 ml (3½ fl oz) fish sauce
250 ml (9 fl oz) coconut milk

3 red chillies, halved and seeded
1 x 200 g (7 oz) piece pork neck
1 teaspoon fennel seeds
1 teaspoon sea salt
¼ pineapple, peeled and chopped into
 bite-sized pieces
Thai basil leaves

Heat a heavy-based pan and add the coconut cream or vegetable oil. If using the coconut cream, keep cooking and stirring until it splits before you add the curry paste. If using the oil, fry the paste until fragrant and the oil is released.

Add the palm sugar and fish sauce, and stir until the sugar dissolves. Add the coconut milk and bring the mixture to the boil, then lower the heat to a simmer. Add the chillies and lower the heat.

Rub the pork with fennel seeds and salt. Grill the pork for 5 minutes over a medium to high heat on each side. Remove from the heat and allow to rest for 10 minutes.

Bring the curry back to a simmer and add the pineapple.

Slice the pork thinly and add to the curry. Stir to combine and add the basil. Spoon into serving bowls and serve.

Braised Duck with Red Curry

100 ml (3½ fl oz) vegetable oil

4 tablespoons Light Red Curry Paste (see
    page 155)

5 kaffir lime leaves

100 g (3½ oz) palm sugar, shaved

150 ml (5 fl oz) fish sauce

1½ tablespoons tamarind

1 kaffir lime, halved

4 long red chillies, seeded and roughly
    chopped

3 stalks water spinach, cut into 3 cm (1¼ in)
    lengths

kaffir lime leaf, julienned

Duck Braise

1 x 1.5 kg (3 lb) duck, halved

1 litre (1¾ pt) coconut milk

1 litre (1¾ pt) Chicken Stock (see page 65)

1 stalk lemongrass, sliced

5 kaffir lime leaves, torn

1 x 4 cm (1½ in) piece galangal, peeled
    and sliced

150 ml (5 fl oz) fish sauce

TO MAKE THE DUCK BRAISE, preheat the oven to 180°C. Rinse and clean the duck and remove any excess fat and the parson's nose.

In a deep heavy-based pot, bring the coconut milk and chicken stock to the boil. Add the lemongrass, lime leaves, galangal and fish sauce, then pour over the duck. Cover with baking paper and foil or a lid and place in the oven for 1½ hours or until the duck is cooked.

When done, remove the duck from the stock and rest on a wire rack. Strain the stock and reserve 500 ml (18 fl oz) for use in the curry. Allow the stock to settle and skim the fat off the top.

Heat the vegetable oil in a heavy-based pan and fry the curry paste and the lime leaves until fragrant. Add the palm sugar and fish sauce. When the sugar dissolves and caramelises slightly, add the reserved 500 ml (18 fl oz) braising liquid and tamarind, and bring to the boil.

Check the seasoning – it should taste sweet, salty, sour and hot. Lower the heat and simmer.

Cut the duck down the back bone and remove the ribcage with your fingers. It should come away easily from the flesh if the duck has been braised for long enough. Discard the bone and cut each duck half into 6 pieces, giving 12 altogether. Add the duck to the curry with the kaffir lime and chilli pieces and simmer for a further 5 minutes.

Add the water spinach and simmer for a further 5 minutes, then spoon into serving dishes.

Garnish with lime leaves, and serve with steamed jasmine rice.

Light Red Curry of Angus Beef

ANY CUT OF BEEF MAY BE USED FOR THIS CURRY, SUCH AS TENDER BEEF CHUCK, BEEF SHIN OR OXTAIL.
YOU WILL NEED TO RESERVE THE BRAISING JUICES FOR THE CURRY. THIS IS GREAT SERVED WITH FRESH RICE
NOODLES OR JASMINE RICE.

SERVES 4

1 x 200 g (7 oz) piece braising beef
500 ml (18 fl oz) coconut milk
1 stalk lemongrass, bruised along its length
2 kaffir lime leaves
1 x 3 cm (1¼ in) piece galangal, peeled
    and sliced
100 g (3½ oz) palm sugar, shaved
100 ml (3½ fl oz) fish sauce
100 ml (3½ fl oz) oyster sauce

Curry
250 ml (9 fl oz) coconut cream
4 tablespoons Red Curry Paste (see
    page 154)
100 g (3½ oz) palm sugar, shaved
100 ml (3½ fl oz) fish sauce
5 kaffir lime leaves
4 red chillies, halved, seeded and julienned
15 g (½ oz) Thai basil leaves
50 ml (1¾ fl oz) light soy sauce
100 g (3½ oz) rice noodles, cut into
    0.5 cm (⅛ in) strips
Thai basil leaves
fresh red chillies, julienned

In a hot pan seal the beef until brown on all sides. Place in a deep baking dish and set aside.

Combine the coconut milk, lemongrass, lime leaves, galangal, palm sugar, fish and oyster sauces in a large saucepan. Bring to the boil and pour over the beef. If there is leftover liquid, reserve for a later use. Cover the braising dish with a lid or seal with baking paper and foil. (I always put baking paper on first so that the foil does not react with the sauce.) Braise for about 2 hours over a low heat.

When done, remove the meat from the juices, set aside to cool, then refrigerate for 2–3 hours. Reserve 300 ml (10 fl oz) of the braising liquid.

TO MAKE THE CURRY, heat the coconut cream in a heavy-based pan until it splits. Add the curry paste and fry until fragrant, about 5 minutes. Add the palm sugar and fish sauce. When the sugar dissolves, add the reserved beef braising liquid and bring to the boil.

Take the beef out of the refrigerator – the meat becomes extremely soft when cooked, and refrigeration helps to firm the meat, making it easier to cut. Slice into 1 cm (⅓ in) pieces.

Add the lime leaves and the beef to the curry. Simmer for 4–5 minutes with the lid on, then add the chilli, basil and soy sauce. The curry should be rich in flavour from the meat stock, and taste salty and sweet. Add the rice noodles and let them soften in the liquid.

Spoon into serving bowls, and sprinkle with extra basil and chilli.

Muslim Curry of Chicken

SERVES 4

200 ml (7 fl oz) fresh coconut cream or
    100 ml (3½ fl oz) vegetable oil
4 tablespoons Muslim-style Curry Paste
    (see page 155)
1 star anise
1 x 2.5 cm (1 in) piece cassia bark
2 bay leaves
2 cardamom pods
6 chicken drumsticks, halved
a little fish sauce
1 litre (1¾ pt) vegetable oil, for deep-frying

4 Nicola or other waxy potatoes, peeled
    and halved
6 pickling onions, peeled
250 ml (9 fl oz) Chicken Stock (see page 65)
250 ml (9 fl oz) coconut cream
100 g (3½ oz) palm sugar, shaved
100 ml (3½ fl oz) fish sauce
2½ tablespoons tamarind
2 tablespoons roasted peanuts, crushed
coriander leaves

Heat a heavy-based pan and add the coconut cream or vegetable oil. If using the coconut cream, keep cooking and stirring until it splits before you add the curry paste with the star anise, cassia bark, bay leaves and cardamom. If using the oil, fry the paste with the star anise, cassia bark, bay leaves and cardamom until fragrant and the oil is released. Set aside.

Toss the chicken with a splash of fish sauce.

Heat the vegetable oil in a wok to just before smoking and deep-fry the chicken pieces until golden brown. Remove and drain.

In the same oil fry the potatoes and onions until golden brown. Remove and drain.

Combine the stock and coconut cream in a heavy-based pot and bring to the boil. Add the chicken and simmer until cooked through, 35–40 minutes. Add the potatoes and onions and allow to cook through, but not to soften completely as they will be cooked in the curry as well. Strain the liquid, reserving the potatoes, onions and chicken and about half the stock.

Place the curry paste back on the heat and moisten with the reserved stock base. Place the chicken, potatoes and onions in the curry, add the palm sugar and fish sauce, and simmer.

Add the tamarind, stir through and taste for seasoning – it should be rich, spicy, sweet and salty.

Spoon into a serving bowl and serve topped with peanuts and coriander.

Spiced Curry of Poussin with Chilli

SERVES 4

1.5 litres (2¾ pt) coconut milk
1 stalk lemongrass, bruised along its length
6 coriander roots, scraped and cleaned
100 ml (3½ fl oz) fish sauce
100 g (3½ oz) palm sugar, shaved
1 poussin
100 g (3½ oz) palm sugar, shaved
100 ml (3½ fl oz) fish sauce
1 large red chilli, roasted and peeled
50 g (1¾ oz) peanuts, roasted and crushed
juice of ½ mandarin
fried peanuts
1 bunch coriander leaves
1½ tablespoons coconut cream

Curry Paste
12 long dried chillies, seeded
225 g (8 oz) sliced red onions
150 g (5½ oz) peeled garlic cloves
2 stalks lemongrass, white part only,
    finely sliced
6 coriander roots, scraped and cleaned
1 x 4 cm (1½ in) piece galangal, peeled
    and finely sliced
2 teaspoons shrimp paste, roasted
1 teaspoon sea salt
1½ tablespoons coriander seeds
1½ tablespoons blade mace
1 teaspoon cumin seeds
3 cardamom pods
3 cloves
1 teaspoon white peppercorns

Bring the coconut milk to the boil in a heavy-based pot. Add the lemongrass, coriander roots, fish sauce and palm sugar. Wash the poussin and place in the coconut milk. Bring to the boil, lower the heat and poach for 25 minutes. Remove the bird and reserve 300 ml (10 fl oz) of the braising liquid. Allow the bird to cool. Halve and remove the centre bones.

TO MAKE THE CURRY PASTE, first soak the chillies in warm water for about 10 minutes.

Place a wok over a medium heat and dry-roast the onions and garlic, adding a little water to prevent burning. When slightly coloured, after 5–10 minutes, add the lemongrass, coriander roots and galangal. Cover the wok to help the cooking process, stirring occasionally until the garlic has softened and cooked through. Add the drained chillies, shrimp paste and salt to the wok and stir well to combine. Take off the heat.

In another wok or pan, roast the coriander, mace, cumin, cardamom and cloves until fragrant. Combine with the peppercorns and grind to a fine powder.

Blend the curry paste in a food processor to a fine paste, then add the ground spices.

Heat a little oil in a pan and fry the curry paste for 10–12 minutes until fragrant and the paste smells cooked. Season with palm sugar and fish sauce, and add the reserved braising liquid. Bring to the boil, add the poussin and chilli. Simmer for 5–10 minutes, then add the peanuts and mandarin juice. Transfer to a serving platter and garnish with extra fried peanuts, coriander and a little coconut cream.

Yellow Curry of Chicken & Sweet Potato

SERVES 4

250 ml (9 fl oz) coconut cream
80 ml (2³/₄ fl oz) Yellow Curry Paste (see
    page 156)
4 jointed chicken leg and thigh, quartered,
    skin on
100 g (3½ oz) palm sugar, shaved

100 ml (3½ fl oz) fish sauce
400 ml (14 fl oz) coconut milk
200 g (7 oz) sweet potato, peeled and
    cut into bite-sized pieces
1 quantity Cucumber Relish (see page 158)

Place the coconut cream in a heavy-based pot on a medium heat and boil until it splits. Add the curry paste and fry until fragrant and you can smell the spices.

Add the chicken and continue to fry until the chicken pieces take on colour. Add the palm sugar and fish sauce, stirring continuously until the sugar is dissolved. Pour over the coconut milk and bring to the boil, reduce and simmer for 15 minutes.

Add the sweet potato and continue to simmer until it is easily pierced by a skewer. This should allow the chicken enough time to cook through. Leave to rest on the stove with the heat off for 15 minutes to help the flavours develop.

Before serving, check the seasoning: it should taste sweet, salty and aromatic. Serve with the cucumber relish.

Jungle Curry of Monkfish & Coriander

THIS CURRY IS ALSO DELICIOUS MADE WITH MINCED DUCK OR RABBIT.

SERVES 4

1 x 250 g (8 oz) fillet monkfish
1 clove garlic, peeled
2 green bird's eye chillies
100 ml (3½ fl oz) vegetable oil
1½ tablespoons chopped lesser galangal
2½ tablespoons Jungle Curry Paste (see page 153)
4 kaffir lime leaves
10 pea aubergines
100 ml (3½ fl oz) fish sauce
½ teaspoon caster (superfine) sugar
1½ tablespoons oyster sauce

300 ml (10 fl oz) Chicken Stock (see page 65) or fish stock
2 small, round Thai aubergines
2 long green chillies, seeded and cut into 2.5 cm (1 in) lengths
2 yard-long beans, cut into 2.5 cm (1 in) lengths
3 baby corn, cut lengthwise
15 g (½ oz) holy basil leaves
10 g (¼ oz) finely shredded flat-leaf coriander
2 tablespoons crisp-fried shallots

Hand-chop the fish to a rough mince.

In a mortar and pestle, pound the garlic and chillies until a uniform paste.

Heat the oil in a wok until just smoking. Add the garlic paste and lesser galangal and fry until light brown and it smells nutty. Add the curry paste and fry until fragrant and the oil is released from the paste.

Add the lime leaves and pea aubergines. Season with fish sauce, sugar and oyster sauce.

Add the stock and simmer for 1–2 minutes, then add the Thai aubergines and chillies. Taste for seasoning – it should be hot and salty at this point, with the sugar just balancing the saltiness.

Add the yard-long beans, baby corn and the minced fish. When you put the fish in, stir so that it doesn't clump together. Simmer for 1 minute, then add the basil. Remove from the heat and spoon onto a serving plate.

Garnish with coriander and shallots, and serve.

Green Curry of Prawns

THE PORK NECK FROM THE RECIPE FOR PINEAPPLE CURRY OF GRILLED PORK (SEE PAGE 77) CAN BE USED IN PLACE OF THE PRAWNS.

SERVES 4

150 ml (5 fl oz) fresh coconut cream or 100 ml (3½ fl oz) vegetable oil
4 tablespoons Green Curry Paste (see page 153)
4 kaffir lime leaves
6 pea aubergines
100 ml (3½ fl oz) fish sauce
100 g (3½ oz) palm sugar, shaved
300 ml (10 fl oz) coconut milk

1 small, round Thai aubergine, sliced
2 long green chillies, seeded and sliced
50 g (1¾ oz) bamboo, sliced
3 baby corn, halved
6 large raw tiger prawns (shrimp), body shell removed and deveined, head and tails left on
15 g (½ oz) Thai basil leaves

Heat a heavy-based pan and add the coconut cream or vegetable oil. If using the coconut cream, keep cooking and stirring until it splits before you add the curry paste. If using the oil, fry the paste until fragrant and the oil is released.

Add the lime leaves and pea aubergines and stir into the paste. Add the fish sauce and palm sugar, moisten with coconut milk and bring to the boil. Taste for seasoning – the mixture should be hot, salty and slightly sweet. Add more seasoning at this point if needed.

Add the Thai aubergines, chillies, bamboo, corn and prawns. Reduce the heat to a simmer and continue to cook for 3 minutes. Fold or stir through the basil, remove from the heat and spoon into a serving bowl. Serve with steamed jasmine rice.

Seafood

Salt & Pepper Cuttlefish with Sweet Soy

Serves 4

2 litres (3½ pt) vegetable oil
250 g (8 oz) cleaned cuttlefish or squid
100 g (3½ oz) tapioca flour, for dusting
1 quantity Salt & Pepper Mix (see page 156)
lemon or lime wedges
Sweet Soy & Ginger Dressing (see page 152)
coriander leaves

Batter
100 g (3½ oz) rice flour
100 g (3½ oz) glutinous rice flour
100 g (3½ oz) tapioca flour
200 ml (7 fl oz) soda water

TO MAKE THE BATTER, sift all the flours into a bowl, then slowly whisk in the soda water to make a thick creamy consistency like pouring cream.

Heat the oil in a wok or a suitably large pan until just smoking.

Score the underside of the cuttlefish in a cross-hatch pattern, then cut into 5 mm (⅛ in) strips. Dip the cuttlefish into the flour to dust, then into the batter.

Holding onto one end of the cuttlefish, dip half of it into the hot oil for 10 seconds. Then let it fall into the oil. This way, the cuttlefish will not stick to the bottom of the pan and instead will float immediately back to the surface. Fry until the batter turns a light golden colour, 4–5 minutes, then remove and drain on absorbent paper.

Continue until all the cuttlefish are done. Dust with the Salt & Pepper Mix.

Place on a serving plate with lemon or lime wedges and a small bowl of the dressing. Garnish with coriander.

Salt & Pepper Crab

SERVES 4 AS PART OF A SHARED MEAL

1 kg (2 lb) crab, cut into 6 pieces
a splash of fish sauce
100 g (3½ oz) tapioca flour
vegetable oil

1 quantity Salt & Pepper Mix (see page 156)
red chillies, finely sliced
Sweet Soy & Ginger Dressing (see page 152)

Toss the crab in the fish sauce, then dust with the tapioca flour.

Heat the oil in a wok until just smoking and add the crab. Cook until the shells turn red and the crab is cooked, about 4 minutes. Remove and drain on absorbent paper.

Dust the crab with the Salt & Pepper Mix. Garnish with the chillies, and serve with a small bowl of the dressing.

Grilled Stuffed Squid

You can use dried or fresh black (wood-ear) fungus for this dish. If using the dried, soak to reconstitute.

Serves 4

2 cloves garlic, peeled
4 coriander roots, scraped and cleaned
½ teaspoon white peppercorns, ground
1 teaspoon sea salt
100 g (3½ oz) black fungus, sliced into thin strips
8 water chestnuts, diced
200 g (7 oz) pork mince
1 teaspoon caster (superfine) sugar
2 teaspoons fish sauce
8 small to medium-sized squid
coriander leaves

peanuts

Salad
100 g (3½ oz) Carrot and Daikon Mix (see page 158)
10 Vietnamese mint leaves
15 g (½ oz) coriander leaves
12 g (⅓ oz) mint leaves
2 tablespoons roasted peanuts, ground

In a mortar and pestle, pound the garlic, coriander roots, peppercorns and salt together.

Mix the pounded ingredients, black fungus and water chestnuts into the pork mince with the sugar and fish sauce. Combine all the ingredients together and mix well to expel all the air. Set aside.

Clean the squid by pulling out the tentacles and ink sac. Reserve the tentacles, discarding the ink and the beak. Wash out the squid tube, peel off the skin and discard. Cut off the wings and reserve for another use.

Fill the squid tube with the pork mince, making a small incision at the point of the tube to expel any air. Fill to about three-quarters full as the stuffing will expand as it cooks. Close the opening with some wooden toothpicks.

Set a steamer over boiling water and steam the squid tubes for 5 minutes until just cooked – this is the best stage to remove them if you are making them in advance. Remove from the steamer.

Heat a barbecue or grill and place the squid tubes on it to caramelise the outside and to give some colour. Barbecue or grill the reserved tentacles to serve with the finished dish.

TO MAKE THE SALAD, toss the ingredients together to mix well. Place on a serving platter.

To serve, slice the tubes on a diagonal and place on top of the salad along with the grilled tentacles. Garnish with extra coriander and peanuts, and serve.

Deep-fried Perch with Three-flavoured Sauce

BABY SNAPPER, WHITING OR RIVER TROUT WORKS WELL IN THIS DISH.

SERVES 4

1 x 800 g (1¾ lb) perch, left whole
vegetable oil
15 g (½ oz) holy basil leaves
2 kaffir lime leaves, julienned
1 large red chilli, julienned
lime wedges

Three-flavoured Sauce
1 coriander root, scraped and cleaned
1 x 2.5 cm (1 in) piece turmeric, peeled
2 red bird's eye chillies
3 long red chillies, seeded
3 red shallots, peeled
1 teaspoon roasted shrimp paste
1½ tablespoons chopped lesser galangal
vegetable oil
200 g (7 oz) palm sugar, shaved
50 g (1¾ oz) tamarind
1½ tablespoons sea salt or fish sauce
100 g (3½ oz) fresh pineapple, peeled
     and diced

TO MAKE THE THREE-FLAVOURED SAUCE, pound the coriander root, turmeric, chillies, shallots, shrimp paste and wild ginger in a mortar and pestle until a uniform paste is achieved.

Heat a little oil in a pan and fry the paste until crisp and fragrant. Add the palm sugar and a tablespoon of water to help dissolve the sugar. Keep cooking until the sugar caramelises slightly, then add the tamarind, salt and pineapple and simmer for about 5 minutes to allow the pineapple to soften. Keep warm.

Score the fish on both sides. Heat the oil in a wok and deep-fry the fish until crisp. Drain on absorbent paper, then transfer to a serving plate. Fry the basil leaves in the oil until crisp. Drain.

Pour the sauce over the fish and garnish with the crisp basil, lime leaves and chilli. Serve with steamed jasmine rice and fresh lime wedges.

Perch Braised with Star Anise & Cassia Bark

THE BRAISING LIQUID USED IN THIS RECIPE IS ALSO DELICIOUS AS A SOUP BROTH. YOU CAN USE A FISH FILLET, BUT WHOLE FISH GIVES THE DISH A BETTER FLAVOUR. DAIKON (MOOLI) IS ANOTHER GOOD ADDITION. YOU COULD ADD HALF A BLANCHED PIG'S TROTTER TO THE BRAISING LIQUID IF YOU WANT A RICHER RESULT.

SERVES 4 AS PART OF A SHARED MEAL

2 coriander roots, scraped and cleaned
2 star anise
2 cloves garlic, peeled and crushed
1 x 2.5 cm (1 in) piece ginger, peeled
½ teaspoon white peppercorns
vegetable oil
50 ml (1¾ fl oz) Chinese cooking wine
2½ tablespoons rock candy, pounded
    to a powder

100 ml (3½ fl oz) oyster sauce
1 litre (1¾ pt) Chicken Stock (see page 65)
    or fish stock
1 x 3 cm (1¼ in) piece cassia bark
1 whole sea perch, cleaned and scaled
a splash of fish sauce
coriander leaves
ground white pepper
crisp-fried garlic

Preheat the oven to 150°C.

Pound the coriander roots, 1 star anise, garlic, ginger and peppercorns in a mortar and pestle to a uniform paste.

Heat a little vegetable oil in a heavy-based pot and fry the paste in as little oil as possible until crisp and fragrant.

Deglaze with the cooking wine, then add the rock candy, oyster sauce and stock. Bring to the boil and skim. Lower the heat to a simmer and taste — it should be sweet, aromatic and salty. Add the cassia bark and remaining star anise. Set aside.

Score the fish on both sides and douse with fish sauce. Drain and place in a braising pan, deep enough to hold all the hot liquid.

Cover the fish with the liquid then cover with baking paper and foil and place in the oven for 20 minutes.

After 20 minutes, remove from the oven and discard the foil and baking paper. Let the fish rest for 10 minutes.

To serve, lift the fish out with 2 spatulas and place on a serving dish. It should be fragrant and a light tan colour.

Bring the braising liquid back to a simmer, check the seasoning and strain enough liquid over the fish to half-cover it. Garnish with coriander, a little pepper and garlic.

In the remaining liquid cook some Chinese broccoli and pea shoots and serve as a side dish. Sprinkle generously with extra crisp-fried garlic and fresh coriander.

Roasted Baby Snapper with Yellow Bean Sauce

1 x 1 kg (2 lb) baby snapper, cleaned and
    scored
3 limes
1 bunch coriander

150 ml (5 fl oz) Yellow Bean Soy Dressing
    (see page 151)
2 red chillies, seeded and julienned

Preheat the oven to 180°C.

Place the fish on oiled baking tray.

Cut 2 limes in half and place in the cavity of the fish with some coriander stalks.

Pour the yellow bean soy dressing over the fish and place in the oven. Bake for 10 minutes.

Open the oven and baste the fish, then increase the temperature to 200°C and bake for a further 5 minutes. The skin should be golden brown and crisp.

Remove the pan from the oven and place the fish on a serving tray. Garnish with the remaining lime, cut into wedges, and chillies. Serve with steamed jasmine rice.

Steamed Snapper with Yellow Bean Soy Dressing

SERVES 4 AS PART OF A SHARED MEAL

100 g (3½ oz) cabbage, shredded
2 spring (green) onions (scallions), cut into
    3 cm (1¼ in) lengths
5 oyster mushrooms
1 x 2.5 cm (1 in) ginger, finely sliced
1 x 800 g (1¾ lb) snapper, left whole and
    scored on both sides

150 ml (5 fl oz) Yellow Bean Soy Dressing
    (see page 151)
200 ml (7 fl oz) Chicken Stock (see
    page 65) or fish stock
15 g (½ oz) coriander leaves, for garnish
½ teaspoon ground white pepper
finely sliced ginger

Place the cabbage, spring onions, mushrooms, ginger and snapper in a deep plate or bowl.

Reserve 1 tablespoon of the yellow bean soy dressing for garnish and combine the rest with the stock in a saucepan. Bring to the boil and pour over the fish.

Set a steamer large enough to hold the plate over boiling water. Place the bowl with the fish in the steamer and cook for 15 minutes.

Check the fish after 15 minutes. If flesh comes away easily from the bone the snapper is ready.

Mix the coriander leaves, pepper and ginger with the reserved yellow bean soy dressing and pour over the fish. Serve with steamed jasmine rice.

Stir-fried Crab with Chilli Jam

DELICIOUS AS AN INDULGENT MEAL FOR TWO. SERVE WITH STEAMED RICE.

SERVES 2

1 x 1 kg (2 lb) crab
100 ml (3½ fl oz) vegetable oil
2 red chillies, seeded and julienned
2 cloves garlic, peeled and crushed
3 kaffir lime leaves
200 ml (7 fl oz) Chilli Jam (see page 150)

100 ml (3½ fl oz) Chicken Stock (see page 65)
50 ml (1¾ fl oz) oyster sauce
50 ml (1¾ fl oz) fish sauce
50 g (1¾ oz) caster (superfine) sugar
spring (green) onions (scallions)
25 g (1 oz) Thai basil leaves

For best results, steam the crab first. If you buy your crab live, kill it humanely by turning the crab on its back and inserting a knife through the point where the back flaps meet. Leave for 2–3 minutes.

Set a steamer set over boiling water and cook the crab for 7 minutes.

Remove the crab from the steamer. Lift up the flap and remove and discard the dead man's fingers. Cut the crab into 6 pieces. Reserve any liquid from inside the crab and any mustard for adding to the sauce.

Heat the oil in a wok until just smoking. Add the chillies, garlic and lime leaves. Stir-fry for 30 seconds, then add the chilli jam, stock, oyster and fish sauces and sugar and reduce the heat. Toss in the crab and any reserved juices and mustard. Toss to coat the crab completely with the sauce, then add the spring onions and basil. Mix well to combine the flavours. (If the crab is still a little raw, place a lid on the wok and let it cook on a low heat for 2 more minutes.)

Spoon onto a serving plate and serve with steamed jasmine rice.

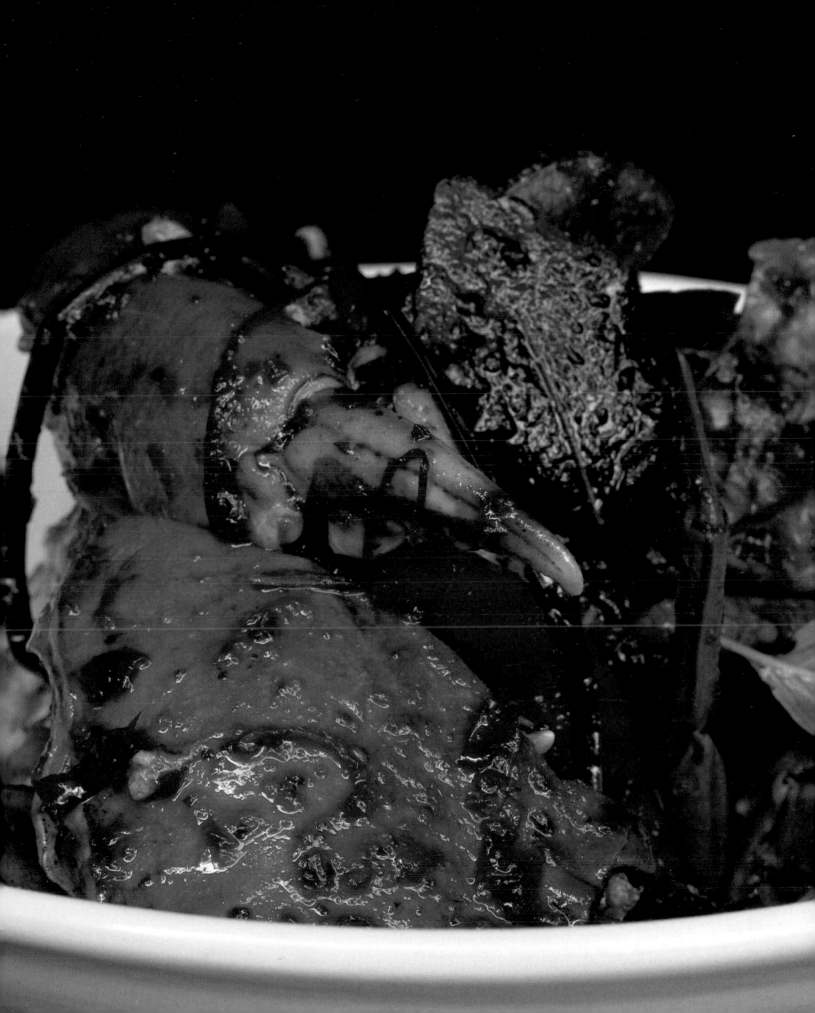

Seared Tuna with Sweet Pork & Kaffir Lime Dressing

SERVES 4 AS PART OF A SHARED MEAL

1 x 200 g (7 oz) fillet tuna
1 quantity Green Chilli Nahm Jim (see
    page 150)
1 kaffir lime, juiced
crisp-fried shallots

Salad
15 g (½ oz) coriander leaves
15 g (½ oz) mint leaves
1 x 3 cm (1¼ in) piece ginger, julienned
1 red chilli, seeded and julienned

Sweet Pork
2 cloves garlic, peeled
2 coriander roots, scraped and cleaned
1 small knob ginger
1 star anise
4 white peppercorns
1 x 200 g (7 oz) piece pork neck
200 ml (7 fl oz) vegetable oil
200 g (7 oz) palm sugar, crushed
100 ml (3½ fl oz) fish sauce
100 ml (3½ fl oz) water

TO MAKE THE SWEET PORK, pound the garlic, coriander roots, ginger, star anise and peppercorns in a mortar and pestle until a uniform paste.

Place the pork neck in a steamer set over boiling water and steam until cooked through, about 20 minutes. Remove and cool. Dice the pork into 1 cm (⅓ in) cubes.

Heat the oil in a wok until just smoking. Fry the pork until golden and crisp. Remove and drain well on absorbent paper.

Pour off half the oil. Heat the remaining oil and fry the paste until it smells nutty and brown. Add the palm sugar and allow to lightly caramelise. Then add the fish sauce and water. Add the pork to the wok, mix and take off the heat.

Heat a pan or grill and sear the tuna in a little oil until rare. Take off the heat and slice into 1 cm (⅓ in) strips. Place on a serving plate, and spoon over the Sweet Pork.

Make the Green Chilli Nahm Jim according to the instructions on page 150, adding the kaffir lime juice for extra flavour.

TO MAKE THE SALAD, combine all the ingredients together, mix well and moisten with the dressing.

Place the salad on the fish and pork, and garnish with some crisp-fried shallots.

Prawns Stir-fried with Turmeric, Chilli & Garlic Paste

SERVES 4 AS PART OF A SHARED MEAL

50 ml (1¾ fl oz) vegetable oil

8 raw tiger prawns (shrimp), body shell
    removed and deveined, head and tails
    left on

2½ tablespoons oyster sauce

1½ tablespoons caster (superfine) sugar

2½ tablespoons fish sauce

150 ml (5 fl oz) Chicken Stock (see page 65)

2 spring (green) onions (scallions), cut into
    2.5 cm (1 in) lengths

1 red chilli, seeded and cut into thin strips

15 g (½ oz) Thai basil leaves

Paste

1 long red chilli

2 cloves garlic, peeled

1 x 1 cm (⅓ in) piece fresh turmeric, peeled

2 coriander roots, scraped and cleaned

1 teaspoon sea salt

TO MAKE THE PASTE, pound all the ingredients in a mortar and pestle until a uniform paste. Heat the oil in a wok or heavy-based frying pan. Add the paste and stir-fry until fragrant.

Add the prawns, toss with paste for 1 minute, then add the oyster sauce, sugar, fish sauce and stock. Taste for seasoning – it should be hot, salty and sweet. Add the spring onions, chilli and basil, stir to mix through and spoon onto a serving dish. Serve with steamed jasmine rice.

Stir-fried Bar Cod with Mange-tout, Ginger & Five Spice

SERVES 4 AS PART OF A SHARED MEAL

500 ml (18 fl oz) vegetable oil

1 x 200 g (7 oz) piece bar cod or white-
    fleshed fish, cut into bite-sized pieces

100 ml (3½ fl oz) fish sauce

100 g (3½ oz) tapioca flour

2 cloves garlic, minced

2 tablespoons julienned ginger

8 mange-tout

1 red chilli, seeded and roughly chopped

2 spring (green) onions (scallions), cut into
    2.5 cm (1 in) lengths

5 Chinese chive flowers

2 stalks Chinese celery, cut into
    2.5 cm (1 in) lengths

50 ml (1¾ fl oz) Chinese cooking wine

2½ tablespoons oyster sauce

50 ml (1¾ fl oz) fish sauce

2½ tablespoons caster (superfine) sugar

100 ml (3½ fl oz) Chicken Stock (see
    page 65)

juice of ½ lemon

1 teaspoon Salt & Pepper Mix (see page 156)

15 g (½ oz) coriander leaves

lemon wedges

Heat the oil in a wok until just smoking.

Toss the fish in the fish sauce, then roll in the flour.

Fry the fish until golden brown, then remove from the oil with a slotted spoon and drain on absorbent paper. Set aside.

Drain off the excess oil, leaving 50 ml (1¾ fl oz) in the wok. Add the garlic and ginger and fry until fragrant. Add the mange-tout, chilli, spring onions, chives and celery, and stir-fry for 2 minutes, then add the fish.

Deglaze the wok with Chinese cooking wine and add oyster and fish sauces, sugar and stock. Toss through and taste for seasoning – it should be salty and sweet. Add the lemon juice and Salt & Pepper Mix.

Toss through half the coriander leaves and spoon onto a serving plate. Garnish with the rest of the coriander and some extra lemon wedges.

Squid with Chinese Celery & Curry Powder

Serves 4

200 g (7 oz) squid tubes
2 cloves garlic, peeled
2 coriander roots, scraped and cleaned
1 x 2.5 cm (1 in) piece ginger, peeled
100 ml (3½ fl oz) vegetable oil
1 white pickling onion, peeled and sliced
2 large red chillies, seeded and chopped
1½ tablespoons Curry Powder (see page 152)
1½ tablespoons fish sauce

1½ tablespoons oyster sauce
1 teaspoon caster (superfine) sugar
100 ml (3½ fl oz) coconut cream
100 ml (3½ fl oz) Chicken Stock (see
    page 65)
1 stalk Chinese celery, finely sliced
2 spring (green) onions (scallions), cut into
    2.5 cm (1 in) lengths
15 g (½ oz) coriander leaves

Cut the squid tubes in half along its length and score the underside in a cross-hatch pattern. Cut each tube into about 8 even-sized pieces.

Pound the garlic, coriander roots and ginger in a mortar and pestle to a uniform paste.

Heat the oil in a wok, add the garlic paste and stir-fry over a medium heat until fragrant.

Add the squid, pickling onion and chillies and stir-fry for a minute. Add the curry powder and stir-fry until all ingredients are an even yellow colour.

Add the fish and oyster sauces, sugar and finally the coconut cream and stock. Taste for seasoning – the mixture should be spicy, salty, sweet and creamy.

Finish off with the celery and spring onions, and fry for a further 30 seconds.

Serve sprinkled with coriander leaves and a dash of coconut cream if desired, and some steamed jasmine rice.

Grilled Fish in a Banana Leaf

CHOOSE FILLETS OF EVEN THICKNESS FOR THIS DISH. IT'S IDEAL FOR BARBECUING. THE YOUNGER THE BANANA LEAF, THE BETTER — IT'S MORE PLIABLE AND EASIER TO WORK WITH. OLDER LEAVES CAN BE BRITTLE, AND WILL NEED BLANCHING BEFORE USE.

SERVES 4 AS PART OF A SHARED MEAL

100 ml (3½ fl oz) vegetable oil
2½ tablespoons Rich Red Curry Paste (see
    page 154)
1½ tablespoons shaved palm sugar
50 ml (1¾ fl oz) fish sauce
1 large piece banana leaf

1 x 200 g (7 oz) fillet sea bass or other
    white-fleshed reef fish
2 kaffir lime leaves, julienned
1 red chilli, seeded and julienned
10 Thai basil leaves
100 ml (3½ fl oz) coconut cream

Heat the oil in a pan to a moderate heat. Add the curry paste and fry until the oil releases from the paste. Add the sugar and fish sauce and taste for seasoning. It should be hot, salty and sweet. Let the paste cool for 5 minutes in a mixing bowl.

Meanwhile, place the banana leaf on a work surface and wipe clean with a damp cloth. If using an older leaf, blanch in boiling water or steam for 2–3 minutes to make it pliable. Cut out the middle rib and discard.

Smear the paste all over the fish and place on the banana leaf. Sprinkle with the lime leaves, chilli, 5 basil leaves and half the coconut cream. Bring the middle and ends of the banana leaf together and secure in the middle with a wooden toothpick.

Set a grill to a medium to high heat. Place the banana leaf parcel on the grill, turning every 2 minutes to ensure even cooking. The length of cooking time depends on the thickness of the fish and the heat of your grill. If you do not have a grill, you can cook the parcel on a tray in an oven preheated to 180°C for about 15 minutes.

Remove the parcel from the heat. Open the banana leaf and place the fish on a serving plate. Garnish with the remaining basil and drizzle over the coconut cream. Serve.

Grilled Sardines with Sweet Fish Sauce

SERVES 4 AS PART OF A SHARED MEAL

6 whole fresh sardines
a splash of fish sauce
50 ml (1¾ fl oz) vegetable oil
crisp-fried garlic
crisp-fried shallots

4 deep-fried long red chillies, seeded
80 ml (2¾ fl oz) Sweet Fish Sauce (see
    page 50)
coriander leaves
lime wedges

To debone the sardines, cut along the underside of the fish. Remove the guts. Wash and place the fish back on the board, belly side up. Gently press down on the fish with your thumb along its length and backbone to flatten. The backbone should now be easily pulled out by breaking the bone closest to the head – gently pull out the backbone and ribcage. Flatten the fish so that it is butterflied, with head and tail still intact. Repeat with the remaining fish.

Place all the fish in a bowl and toss with a splash of fish sauce.

Set a grill to a medium to high heat, lightly oil and place the fish, skin side down, on the grill and cook until a golden brown colour. Carefully flip over with a spatula to seal the other side. Sardines cook quickly, so keep an eye on them.

Place the fish on a serving plate, sprinkle generously with the crisp-fried garlic and shallots. Break the roasted chillies over the top, drizzle with sweet fish sauce and garnish with coriander and lime wedges.

Grilled Tuna with a Chilli, Garlic & Shallot Relish

SERVES 4 AS PART OF A SHARED MEAL

4 x 180 g (6 oz) pieces tuna

Relish
8 cloves garlic, peeled
8 red shallots, peeled
4 red chillies, seeded
1 ripe tomato
1 red pepper, roasted and peeled
2½ tablespoons shaved palm sugar
50 ml (1¾ fl oz) fish sauce
100 ml (3½ fl oz) tamarind

Salad
15 g (½ oz) coriander leaves
10 g (¼ oz) mint leaves
½ stalk lemongrass, white part only, finely
   sliced
100 g (3½ oz) cabbage, finely sliced
¼ cucumber, cut into batons
1 red shallot, peeled and sliced
1 red chilli, seeded and julienned

TO MAKE THE RELISH, dry-roast the garlic, shallots, chillies and tomato in a wok over a medium to high heat until soft and caramelised. Put a lid over the wok to finish the cooking and to allow the ingredients to steam.

Remove the ingredients from the wok. Mix with the red pepper and pound to a rough paste in a mortar and pestle. You may have to do this in batches, depending on the size of your mortar. Stir in the palm sugar, fish sauce and tamarind.

Heat a grill to medium–high. Grill the tuna for about 2 minutes on each side, depending on the thickness of the fish, until rare.

Remove from the heat. Break up the fish and place in a serving dish.

TO MAKE THE SALAD, toss all the ingredients together, adding just enough relish to bind them together.

Place the salad on the fish and serve with extra relish on the side – it is great mixed through hot steamed rice.

Wine & Asian Food

Meat

Braised Beef Shin with a Hot & Sour Salad

THE RICHNESS OF THE MEATY BRAISING LIQUID WILL BE BALANCED BY THE HOT AND SOUR DRESSING IN THE SALAD, GIVING A GOOD BALANCE OF FLAVOURS.

SERVES 4 AS PART OF A SHARED MEAL

Braised Beef
1 x 200 g (7 oz) piece beef shin
1½ tablespoons thick sweet soy sauce
100 ml (3½ fl oz) vegetable oil
5 cloves garlic, peeled
1 x 4 cm (1½ in) piece ginger, peeled
1 coriander root, scraped and cleaned
1 small red onion
100 ml (3½ fl oz) Chinese cooking wine
50 g (1¾ oz) rock candy, crushed
50 ml (1¾ fl oz) oyster sauce
500 ml (18 fl oz) Chicken Stock (see page 65)
50 ml (1¾ fl oz) Chinese black vinegar
1 teaspoon sea salt

Hot & Sour Salad
50 ml (1¾ fl oz) lime juice
½ teaspoon red chilli powder
1½ tablespoons fish sauce
2 green bird's eye chillies, finely sliced
10 coriander leaves
10 mint leaves
1 spring (green) onion (scallion), finely shredded
1 red shallot, peeled and finely sliced
½ large red chilli, seeded and finely sliced

TO MAKE THE BRAISED BEEF, rub the thick sweet soy sauce all over the beef. Heat a little vegetable oil in a pan and seal the beef on all sides. Place in a deep braising pan.

Pound the garlic, ginger, coriander root and onion to a paste. Heat some oil in a heavy-based saucepan and fry the pounded ingredients until golden brown. Discard the excess oil and deglaze with the Chinese cooking wine. Add the rock candy, oyster sauce and chicken stock. Bring to the boil and skim off all the scum. Pour the liquid over the beef. Cover with greaseproof paper and foil, and braise on top of the stove for 1½ hours until the meat is soft.

Remove the meat and set aside. Strain the liquid and boil hard to reduce by a third. Add the vinegar and salt and taste – the mixture should taste rich and meaty.

TO MAKE THE HOT & SOUR SALAD, combine the lime juice, chilli powder, fish sauce and chillies. This dressing should taste very hot and sour.

In a stainless steel bowl, toss together the rest of the ingredients and add the dressing.

To serve, cut the braised beef into 1 cm (⅓ in) slices and reheat in the reduced braising liquid. Place the sliced beef in the middle of the serving bowl, and pour over a generous amount of the braising liquid.

Place the hot and sour salad on top of the beef, and pour some of the dressing into the meaty juices. Serve with steamed rice.

Barbecue Pork

USE THIS PORK IN STIR-FRIES AND SALADS, OR JUST ENJOY ON ITS OWN WITH JASMINE RICE, SOY SAUCE AND CHILLI. IT'S WORTH HAVING IN THE FRIDGE FOR SNACKS, SO THE QUANTITIES GIVEN HERE ARE GENEROUS.

SERVES 6 AS PART OF A SHARED MEAL

80 ml (2¾ fl oz) fermented bean curd
4 tablespoons light yellow bean soy
100 ml (3½ fl oz) Chinese cooking wine
80 ml (2¾ fl oz) hoisin sauce

4 tablespoons yellow bean paste
5 tablespoons caster (superfine) sugar
4 cloves garlic, peeled
1 x 2 kg (4 lb) piece pork neck, quartered

Mix all the ingredients except the pork together and blend to a smooth paste.

Marinate the pork in the paste for as little as 2 hours or as long as 24 hours – the longer the better.

When you're ready to cook, preheat the oven to 180°C.

Place the pork sections on a cooling rack over an oven dish, and half-fill the dish with water. This will help to stop the meat from drying out during cooking.

Roast the pork for 35–40 minutes or until golden and fragrant. Rest the meat for 10–15 minutes. Slice finely and serve with steamed jasmine rice and some Chinese greens.

Pork, Crab & Beansprout Omelette

SERVES 4

100 ml (3½ fl oz) vegetable oil
4 medium-sized eggs, beaten
150 g (5 oz) cooked pork mince
150 g (5 oz) crabmeat, picked
½ teaspoon ground white pepper
1 teaspoon sea salt

1 x 2.5 cm (1 in) piece ginger, peeled
   and julienned
1 spring (green) onion (scallion), cut into
   fine rounds
55 g (2 oz) beansprouts

Heat the oil in a wok or non-stick pan until just smoking and add the beaten eggs. The mixture will bubble around the edges (if you are using a well-seasoned wok, it will not stick).

Gently move the egg with a spatula to help the egg cook. Add the rest of the ingredients to the middle of the egg. When you have done this, push gently down with the spatula; the egg will ooze out towards the edges. Let the egg brown for 30 seconds, then turn out onto a large serving plate.

This is great served with Cucumber Relish (see page 158).

Braised Beef Ribs with Sweet Fish Sauce

SHIN BEEF ALSO WORKS WELL IN PLACE OF THE BEEF RIBS.

SERVES 4 AS PART OF A SHARED MEAL

1 litre (1¾ pt) vegetable oil
1 kg (2 lb) good quality beef ribs
500 ml (18 fl oz) coconut cream
500 ml (18 fl oz) Chicken Stock (see page 65)
1 x 4 cm (1½ in) piece galangal, peeled and chopped
100 ml (3½ fl oz) oyster sauce
4 kaffir lime leaves
1 stalk lemongrass

100 ml (3½ fl oz) fish sauce
100 g (3½ oz) palm sugar, shaved
100 ml (3½ fl oz) Sweet Fish Sauce (see page 50)
1 red shallot, peeled and sliced
coriander leaves
mint leaves
flat-leaf coriander, shredded
Nahm Pla Prik (see page 152)

Preheat the oven to 180°C/gas 4.

Heat the vegetable oil in a wok and shallow-fry the ribs until brown and caramelised. Drain and place in a deep braising pan.

In a heavy-based pot, combine the coconut cream, stock, galangal, oyster sauce, lime leaves and lemongrass and bring to the boil. Season with fish sauce and palm sugar. We're looking for a tasty base – after using it for braising, the liquid can be reduced for use as a sauce or as a base for a curry.

Pour the braising liquid over the beef, cover with a lid or baking paper and foil and braise for 1½–2 hours. Let the ribs cool in the liquid.

Remove the ribs from the stock. Strain and reserve the liquid. You could season it, and shred the beef back into the liquid and serve as a soup.

Set a grill to a medium to high heat. Grill the ribs until caramelised on the outside. Place the ribs on a serving plate and drizzle over the sweet fish sauce and garnish with the shallots, coriander, mint and flat-leaf coriander. Serve with the Nahm Pla Prik.

Stir-fried Beef with Black Beans & Pickled Mustard Greens

SERVES 4 AS PART OF A SHARED MEAL

4 tablespoons vegetable oil

1½ tablespoons grated ginger

2 cloves garlic, peeled and finely chopped

200 g (7 oz) beef rump, finely sliced

4 tablespoons Chinese cooking wine

1½ tablespoons Black Bean Sauce (see page 152)

100 ml (3½ fl oz) Chicken Stock (see page 65)

1½ tablespoons caster (superfine) sugar

1 piece pickled mustard green, sliced

10 mange-tout

2 red chillies, seeded and chopped

coriander leaves

Heat the oil in a wok until just smoking and fry the ginger and garlic until nutty and fragrant. Add the beef and stir-fry until it changes colour. Deglaze with the Chinese cooking wine and add the black bean sauce.

Add the chicken stock and sugar, then add the mustard greens, mange-tout and chilli. Stir-fry for 2 minutes until all the ingredients are well coated and cooked through.

Taste for seasoning – it should be salty and sweet. There should be some liquid for sauce; if too dry, add a little more chicken stock or water. Taste for seasoning, adjusting as necessary.

Remove from the heat and transfer to a serving plate. Garnish with coriander.

Pork & Peanut Sausage

You can purchase sausage casing (pigs' intestines) from your butcher. If you are making these sausages in advance, omit the basil leaves, as they tend to blacken if left for more than a few hours before cooking.

Serves 4 as part of a shared meal

300 g (10 oz) lean pork mince
300 g (10 oz) fatty pork mince
100 g (3½ oz) Peanut Curry Paste (see
    page 154)
5 kaffir lime leaves, finely shredded
2½ tablespoons sea salt
150 g (5 oz) palm sugar, crushed

100 g (3½ oz) roasted peanuts, crushed
25 g (1 oz) Thai basil leaves, roughly chopped
1 metre (about 1 yard) pigs' intestines,
    cleaned and rinsed thoroughly
vegetable oil
banana leaf

Combine both types of pork mince in a large mixing bowl. Add the curry paste, lime leaves and salt and mix well together. Add the palm sugar, then the peanuts and basil. Mix well together and pick up small handfuls of the mixture and throw it back into the mixing bowl. Repeat this process for about 5 minutes so that all possible air is expelled. Before you pipe the mixture, fry a little of the filling in vegetable oil to check the seasoning.

Wash the intestines well. Push one end over the spout of a tap and slowly run some cold water through it to check for holes.

Spoon the pork mixture into a piping bag with a nozzle attached, then place the intestine over the nozzle. When the entire intestine has been fed on, tie a knot at one end of the intestine and start piping the mix, sliding the intestine off the nozzle as it fills with the mixture. Coil the sausage into a spiral and place on a stainless or plastic tray as you go along. There should be enough mixture to make a sausage to fill a small steamer, about 20 cm (4 in) across. Brush the sausage with some vegetable oil so it won't dry out.

Set a steamer over boiling water and place the sausage on a piece of banana leaf. Poke a few holes in it with a skewer so the sausages won't split when cooking. Steam for 10 minutes, then remove the sausage and let it cool slightly.

You can prepare the sausage in advance until this stage. To keep, brush with some oil and refrigerate.

To cook the sausage, place on a preheated grill and cook the sausage until the skin is caramelised and smells fragrant, 4–6 minutes. Remove from the heat and rest for 5–10 minutes.

To serve, cut the sausage at an angle. The sausages are great on their own or served on a betel leaf with some fresh chilli and finely sliced ginger. Or make a salad with some ginger, coriander and red shallots, tossed with a simple dressing of sweet chilli sauce and lime juice.

Caramelised Pork Hock with Chilli Vinegar

FOR A COMPLETE DISH TO HAVE WITH RICE, STEAM SOME CHINESE BROCCOLI AND PLACE IT UNDERNEATH THE PORK HOCK.

SERVES 6–8

vegetable oil for deep-frying
2 pork hocks
1 quantity Master Stock (see page 65)
crisp-fried shallots
coriander leaves
red chilli, julienned
½ quantity Chilli Vinegar (see page 151)

Caramel
500 g (1 lb) palm sugar, crushed
1 stick cassia bark
1 star anise

Heat the oil in a wok until just smoking and deep-fry the pork hock, one at a time, until golden brown, 4–5 minutes. Remove from the oil and drain well on absorbent paper.

Bring the Master Stock to the boil in a large heavy-based pan. Add the pork hocks and simmer for 1½–2 hours over a medium heat. To test for readiness, the pork hocks should be quite soft to the touch. Remove the hocks from the stock and cool. Reserve 1 cup of the braising liquid for the sauce.

When cool, grab the hock bone and twist – the whole bone should come out, leaving only the meat. Push the hock together to form a dense mass and refrigerate until set and firm, 3–4 hours.

TO MAKE THE CARAMEL, place the palm sugar in a heavy-based pot and add a splash of water to help it melt. Allow the sugar to caramelise, then stop the cooking by adding the reserved braising liquid, cassia bark and star anise to give it a good flavour. The caramel should be quite savoury and not too runny – a honey-like consistency. If too runny, keep reducing the stock until a sauce consistency. Check the seasoning: if it's too sweet, add 100 ml (3½ fl oz) of fish sauce to cut the sweetness.

To serve, cut the pork hock into bite-sized pieces.

Reheat the previous oil in a wok and deep-fry the meat until crisp and golden, 5–6 minutes. Drain on absorbent paper.

To serve, place in a bowl and pour over the warm caramel. Garnish with some crisp-fried shallots, coriander and chilli. Serve with Chilli Vinegar on the side.

Grilled Pork Neck with Fennel Seeds

THE PORK FROM THIS RECIPE CAN ALSO BE COOKED INTO A GREEN CURRY.

Serves 4

2 teaspoons fennel seeds

2 teaspoons sea salt

1 x 200 g (7 oz) piece pork neck

2½ tablespoons thick sweet soy sauce

Pound the fennel and salt to a fine powder in a mortar and pestle. Rub into the pork neck and let sit for 1 hour in the refrigerator.

Set a grill on a medium to high heat.

Rub the thick sweet soy sauce into the meat, then grill on all sides for 8–10 minutes until well caramelised and fragrant, taking care not to burn the outside or the burnt spice will turn bitter.

Rest for 10 minutes before slicing and serving.

Soy-braised Suckling Pig

YOU'LL HAVE TO PRE-ORDER THE SUCKLING PIG FROM A BUTCHER. FLAVOUR THE MASTER STOCK WITH LOTS OF AROMATICS SO THAT THE PORK SKIN TAKES ON LOTS OF FLAVOUR.

SERVES 4

1 x 800 g (1¾ lb) suckling pig leg
1 quantity Master Stock (see page 65)
vegetable oil for deep-frying

8–10 star anise
2 sticks cassia bark
70 g (2½ oz) sliced ginger

Put the pork leg, Master Stock, spices and ginger in a pan large enough to hold them all, and braise over a medium heat for 25–30 minutes. Allow the leg to cool in the stock.

When cool, remove from the stock and allow the pork leg to dry thoroughly. For the best crisp results, place the pork leg in front of a fan set on low or in a well-ventilated area of the kitchen. If you refrigerate, take out of the refrigerator 1–2 hours before frying so that it warms through to the middle and the skin doesn't burn.

Heat the vegetable oil in a wok until just smoking. Deep-fry the pork until the skin is a deep golden colour and crisp, 5–8 minutes. Remove and drain on absorbent paper.

Slice and serve with Grilled Aubergine & Chilli Relish (see page 157) or Yellow Bean Soy Dressing (see page 151) and rice.

Poultry

Stir-fried Duck with Red Curry & Salted Duck Eggs

USE THE BRAISED DUCK FROM THE RECIPE FOR BRAISED DUCK LEGS WITH CASHEW NUTS, BEANSPROUTS & CHILLI (SEE PAGE 133) FOR THIS DISH.

SERVES 4 AS PART OF A SHARED MEAL

4 cooked jointed duck leg and thigh
1 clove garlic, peeled and crushed
1 red bird's eye chilli
400 ml (14 fl oz) vegetable oil
15 g (½ oz) holy basil
2½ tablespoons chopped lesser galangal
2½ tablespoons Light Red Curry Paste (see page 155)
4 kaffir lime leaves

12 pea aubergines
2 apple aubergines
2 red chillies, seeded and cut into strips
100 ml (3½ fl oz) Chicken Stock (see page 65)
2½ tablespoons oyster sauce
2½ tablespoons fish sauce
1½ tablespoons caster (superfine) sugar
1 salted duck egg, boiled and peeled

Cook the duck following the instructions on page 133. When cooked, cut each jointed duck leg into 2 pieces, separating the thigh and leg.

Pound the garlic and chilli in a mortar and pestle to a uniform paste.

Heat the oil in a wok and fry the duck until golden brown, about 1½ minutes. Remove from the oil and drain on absorbent paper. Fry the basil leves in the oil for 1 minute. Drain.

Remove the oil from the wok, leaving 100 ml (3½ fl oz). Lower the heat to medium, add the garlic and chilli paste and ginger and fry until fragrant. Add the curry paste and lime leaves, and cook until the paste is fragrant and no rawness can be detected.

Add both types of aubergine and chillies and return the duck to the pan. Season with the chicken stock, oyster and fish sauces and sugar, and mix well to combine the flavours. At this point, taste – it should be hot, rich and full flavoured. If the mixture is too dry, add a little more stock.

Break up the egg and toss with the duck. Spoon onto a serving plate and garnish with the fried basil leaves.

Soy Duck or Chicken

This duck or chicken can be used in all of the recipes that call for duck or chicken bought from a Chinese foodstore. It's also good shredded into the Spring Onion Pancakes (see page 158).

Serves 8

1 quantity Master Stock (see page 65)
1 duck or chicken
fresh ginger

1 piece cassia bark
1 star anise
1 pig's trotter

Bring the Master Stock to the boil. If reusing the stock, refresh with extra ginger and spices. (It is good to add extra ginger anyway if cooking chicken.) Add the pig's trotter.

Wash and pat dry the duck or chicken, removing any excess fat and the parson's nose, especially from the duck as there is a gland within that can make the stock bitter.

Chicken will take 45–50 minutes, and the duck will take about 70 minutes to cook over a gentle simmer. Ducks tend to float, too, so you may need to fit a lid that is slightly smaller than the pot over the top to stop the duck from bobbing up.

When done, remove the duck or chicken from the stock and place on a cooling rack.

Before cooking further, for example, deep-frying, place the bird in the refrigerator for the best crisp-skinned results, as the dry, cool air of the fridge will dry out the skin well.

If cooking further, cut the chicken or duck in half and fry, half at a time, to warm the meat all the way through.

Stir-fried Soy Duck with Wingbeans

BUY A READY-PREPARED SOY DUCK FROM CHINATOWN FOR THIS DISH. ASK FOR A CONTAINER OF DUCK JUICES AS WELL. IF YOU'VE COOKED THE DUCK AT HOME, YOU CAN USE THE MASTER STOCK IN PLACE OF THE CHICKEN STOCK.

SERVES 4 AS PART OF A SHARED MEAL

1 Soy Duck (see page 129)
100 ml (3½ fl oz) vegetable oil
2 red chillies, seeded and cut into bite-sized
   pieces
2 cloves garlic, peeled and pounded
1 x 4 cm (1½ in) piece ginger, peeled and
   julienned
100 ml (3½ fl oz) Chinese cooking wine
2 x 2.5 cm (1 in) lengths spring (green)
   onions (scallions)

4 wingbeans, cut into bite-sized pieces
100 ml (3½ fl oz) duck juice or Chicken Stock
   (see page 65)
50 ml (1¾ fl oz) oyster sauce
50 g (1¾ oz) caster (superfine) sugar
50 ml (1¾ fl oz) fish sauce
50 ml (1¾ fl oz) soy sauce
15 g (½ oz) Thai basil

Cut the duck down the middle and remove the rib bones. Cut the leg in half and the breast into quarters. You can get the shop to chop it for you in this way.

Heat the oil in a wok or pan and add the chillies, garlic and ginger. Stir-fry until fragrant for 20 seconds, taking care not to burn the garlic or it will turn bitter.

Deglaze the wok with Chinese cooking wine, add the duck, spring onions and wingbeans. Then add the duck juices or stock, oyster sauce, sugar, fish and soy sauces. Taste – it should be rich and full flavoured. Add the basil to finish. Serve with steamed rice.

Soy Chicken Stir-fried with Lotus Root

LOTUS ROOT IS GREAT FOR ABSORBING ALL THE FLAVOURS FROM THE STIR-FRY. YOU CAN FIND FRESH LOTUS ROOT IN SOME CHINESE GROCERS. THE FROZEN IS ALSO AVAILABLE. IF YOU'VE POACHED YOUR OWN CHICKEN AT HOME, USE SOME OF THE MASTER STOCK IN PLACE OF THE CHICKEN STOCK.

SERVES 4

100 ml (3½ fl oz) vegetable oil
2 red chillies, seeded and cut into strips
2 cloves garlic, peeled and crushed
2 tablespoons finely chopped ginger
a splash of Chinese cooking wine
½ Soy Chicken (see page 129), chopped
　　into pieces
8 mange-tout
8 pieces thinly sliced lotus root

6 oyster mushrooms
100 ml (3½ fl oz) Chicken Stock (see
　　page 65)
2½ tablespoons oyster sauce
2½ tablespoons fish sauce
2½ tablespoons light yellow bean soy
2½ tablespoons caster (superfine) sugar
2 spring (green) onions (scallions), cut into
　　2.5 cm (1 in) lengths

Heat the oil in a wok until just smoking.

Add the chillies, garlic and ginger and fry until fragrant, about 30 seconds. Deglaze with Chinese wine and add the chicken, mange-tout, lotus root and mushrooms. Toss for about 30 seconds, then add the stock, oyster and fish sauces, yellow bean soy and sugar. Add the spring onions and toss for a further 30 seconds. Taste for seasoning – it should be rich and full flavoured.

Spoon onto a serving plate and serve with steamed jasmine rice.

Braised Duck Legs with Cashew Nuts, Beansprouts & Chilli

Yam beans can be used in place of the water chestnuts.

SERVES 4 AS PART OF A SHARED MEAL

1 quantity Master Stock (see page 65)
4 duck legs, trimmed of excess fat
100 ml (3½ fl oz) thick sweet soy sauce
500 ml (18 fl oz) vegetable oil
2½ tablespoons Chinese black vinegar
1 drop sesame oil
1½ tablespoons hoisin sauce

Salad
100 g (3½ oz) beansprouts
15 g (½ oz) coriander leaves
½ x 185 g (6 oz) tin water chestnuts, drained
    and chopped
2 spring (green) onions (scallions), julienned
4 tablespoons roasted cashew nuts, lightly
    crushed
1 red chilli, seeded and julienned
1 x 3 cm (1¼ in) piece ginger, peeled and
    julienned

Bring the Master Stock to the boil. If reusing from another recipe, add some extra ginger, star anise and salt to refresh the stock.

Rub the duck legs with the soy. Heat the oil in a wok and shallow-fry the legs until golden brown, about 2 minutes. Transfer the legs to a braising pan and cover with boiling stock. Braise for 50 minutes on a gentle simmer or until the duck is tender and a rich, deep brown colour. Remove the duck from the braising liquid and cool. Reserve ½ cup of the stock and cool. Taste for seasoning to see how strong it is. If it's too strong in flavour, dilute with a little chicken stock or water.

TO MAKE THE SALAD, combine all the ingredients together in a large bowl.

Take the duck meat off the bone and shred. Toss the meat with the salad, then place on a serving plate.

Add the vinegar, sesame oil and hoisin sauce to the reserved braising liquid to make a dressing and pour over the salad. Serve with steamed jasmine rice.

Spiced Chicken with Plum Sauce

USE FREE-RANGE CHICKENS OR YOU'LL BE DISAPPOINTED WITH THE RESULT.

SERVES 8 AS PART OF A SHARED MEAL

4 star anise
2 sticks cassia bark
100 g (3½ oz) Sichuan peppercorns
4 small dried red chillies
½ cup sea salt
1 free-range chicken
4 litres (3¼ quarts) vegetable oil
1 quantity Salt & Pepper Mix (see page 156)
lemon wedges

Plum Sauce
500 g (1 lb) palm sugar, crushed
100 ml (3½ fl oz) water
100 ml (3½ fl oz) fish sauce
100 ml (3½ fl oz) tamarind
10 plums
100 ml (3½ fl oz) hoisin sauce

Dry-roast the star anise, cassia bark, Sichuan peppercorns and chillies in a heavy-based pan until fragrant. Mix with the salt and grind to a fine powder in a spice or coffee grinder.

Dry the chicken with a kitchen towel, and coat thoroughly with the ground spices.

Set a steamer large enough to hold the chicken over boiling water. Place the bird in the steamer and steam, covered, for 50 minutes on a gentle simmer. When done, remove the chicken and allow to cool to room temperature. You'll notice the spice coating dry and harden, which is essential before it is fried. This can be done in advance.

Heat the vegetable oil in a large wok. Cut the bird in half and fry in the hot oil until the skin is crisp. Drain on absorbent paper.

TO MAKE THE PLUM SAUCE, melt the sugar in a heavy-based pot with the water. Let sugar caramelise slightly, then add the fish sauce and tamarind. Add the plums and hoisin sauce, and cook until they release their juices. Keep cooking until you get a honey-like consistency again. The mixture should taste sweet, slightly sour and salty. Pass the sauce through a wire mesh strainer to make a rich, red sauce. When reheating, add a few slices of fresh plum to the sauce if desired.

To serve, cut the chicken into 6 pieces and place on a serving platter. Spoon over the sauce. Serve the Salt & Pepper Mix on the side. Garnish with lemon wedges.

Stir-fried Chicken with Basil

THIS RECIPE IS ALSO DELICIOUS MADE WITH SLICED BEEF AND BAMBOO SHOOTS.

SERVES 4 AS PART OF A SHARED MEAL

100 ml (3½ fl oz) vegetable oil
200 g (7 oz) chicken breast or thigh fillet,
    sliced
2 red chillies, seeded and cut into 2.5 cm
    (1 in) strips
1 clove garlic, crushed
2½ tablespoons chopped lesser galangal
100 ml (3½ fl oz) Chicken Stock (see
    page 65)

2½ tablespoons oyster sauce
2½ tablespoons fish sauce
1½ tablespoons caster (superfine) sugar
3 yard-long beans, cut into 2.5 cm (1 in)
    lengths
15 g (½ oz) holy basil leaves
red chilli, julienned
kaffir lime leaf, julienned

Heat the oil in a wok until just smoking.

Add the chicken and stir-fry until well coloured. Pour off any excess oil, then toss in the chillies, garlic and lesser galangal. Stir-fry for 30 seconds, then add the stock, oyster and fish sauces, sugar and yard-long beans. Taste for seasoning – it should be rich and full flavoured. Add the basil, which will give a peppery finish to the dish. Toss to combine the flavours, then spoon onto a serving plate. Garnish with some julienned chilli and kaffir lime leaf.

Twice-cooked Poussin with Shredded Coconut

1 poussin

250 ml (9 fl oz) coconut cream

2 stalks lemongrass, bruised along its length

1½ tablespoons tamarind

1 teaspoon crushed palm sugar

2 slices galangal

flesh of ½ coconut, shredded

2 large red chillies, seeded and julienned

15 g (½ oz) Thai basil leaves

Spice Paste

3 large red chillies

½ teaspoon shrimp paste, roasted in foil

2 cloves garlic, peeled

3 red shallots, peeled

4 slices galangal

Cut the poussin down the breast bone and open it out in one flat piece. Skewer the legs down to the back so the bird remains flat during first cooking.

TO MAKE THE SPICE PASTE, pound all the ingredients to a uniform paste in a mortar and pestle. Rub the paste into the bird.

Place the coconut cream, lemongrass, tamarind, sugar and galangal in a heavy-based pot large enough to hold the flat bird. Add the bird and remaining spice paste and simmer gently with the lid off.

Baste the bird constantly during cooking if not totally submerged, until tender, about 20 minutes. Remove the bird from the steamer and cool or refrigerate. Reserve the braising liquid.

Heat a chargrill and roast the bird over a very low heat until the outside is golden and caramelised, about 8 minutes. You can also caramelise the outside under a griller.

Remove the skewer and cut the bird in half and place on a serving plate.

Add the coconut, chillies and basil to the reserved braising liquid and taste for seasoning, adjusting if necessary. Pour the mixture over the grilled bird and serve.

Desserts

Durian Pancakes

DURIAN ARE A TROPICAL FRUIT KNOWN FOR THEIR STRONG SMELL AND SWEET CUSTARDY TEXTURE. THEY ARE AVAILABLE FROM CHINESE AND THAI FOODSHOPS. IF UNAVAILABLE, REPLACE WITH ONE MORE BANANA.

MAKES 12

90 g (3¼ oz) grated coconut flesh
140 g (5 oz) rice flour
50 g (1¾ oz) tapioca flour
1½ tablespoons arrowroot flour
2 ripe bananas, mashed
50 g (1¾ oz) durian
170 g (6 oz) palm sugar, shaved

1 medium-sized egg
250 ml (9 fl oz) coconut cream
vegetable oil
120 ml (4 fl oz) Palm Sugar Caramel (see page 159)
Passionfruit Ice-cream (see page 142)

Mix the coconut flesh with the flours.

In a separate bowl mash the bananas and durian, then add the palm sugar, egg and coconut cream and mix well with a wooden spoon. Pour into a blender and process until the mixture is smooth.

Pour this mixture into the flour and coconut mixture, whisking until a smooth batter is achieved. Cover and let stand in the refrigerator for at least 1 hour.

Heat a non-stick pan until medium hot. Brush the surface with a little oil and spoon on some batter. Let the mixture bubble and brown as you would a normal pancake, then turn over and allow to lightly brown on the other side. Repeat with the remaining batter.

Place the pancakes on a serving plate and serve with the Palm Sugar Caramel and some Passionfruit Ice-cream.

Palm Sugar Ice-cream

MAKES 1 LITRE (1³/₄ PT)

500 ml (18 fl oz) coconut cream
200 ml (7 fl oz) milk
8 egg yolks

100 g (7 oz) caster (superfine) sugar
100 ml (3½ fl oz) Palm Sugar Caramel (see page 159)

Combine the coconut cream and milk in a heavy-based saucepan and bring to the boil.

In a mixing bowl, beat the egg yolks and sugar until pale and thick. While stirring, pour the coconut cream mixture into the egg mixture and whisk together. Return the mixture to the saucepan over a medium heat and stir with a wooden spoon until the mixture coats the back of a wooden spoon. Remove from the heat and allow to cool completely.

Stir in the palm sugar caramel and churn the mixture in an ice-cream machine according to the manufacturer's instructions.

Passionfruit Ice-cream

MAKES 1 LITRE (1³/₄ PT)

500 ml (18 fl oz) coconut cream
200 ml (7 fl oz) milk
8 egg yolks

200 g (7 oz) caster (superfine) sugar
100 ml (3½ fl oz) fresh passionfruit pulp

Combine the coconut cream and milk in a heavy-based saucepan and bring to the boil.

In a mixing bowl, beat the egg yolks and sugar until pale and thick. While stirring, pour the coconut cream mixture into the egg mixture and whisk together. Return the mixture to the saucepan over a medium heat and stir with a wooden spoon until the mixture coats the back of a wooden spoon. Remove from the heat and allow to cool completely.

Stir in the passionfruit pulp and churn the mixture in an ice-cream machine according to the manufacturer's instructions.

Caramel Custard with Grilled Banana

The addition of fresh turmeric in the caramel gives it a golden colour and the pandanus leaf a fresh, grassy taste. Two types of palm sugar are used for the caramel in this dish: black palm sugar is an Indonesian gula jawa; the other is paler and has a less smoky flavour. All are available from Chinese and Thai foodstores. You will need 6 x 180 ml (6 fl oz) ramekins for this dish.

SERVES 6

6 ripe bananas
4 tablespoons Palm Sugar Caramel (see
    page 159), extra
coconut cream

Custard
6 duck eggs
500 ml (18 fl oz) coconut cream
1 teaspoon sea salt
375 ml (13 fl oz) Palm Sugar Caramel
    (see page 159)

Preheat the oven to 150°C/gas 2. Place the ramekins in a shallow baking tray.

TO MAKE THE CUSTARD, combine all the ingredients together in a mixing bowl. Mix well, then strain into a jug with a pouring lip. Pour the custard into the ramekins. To ensure a smooth top on the finished caramel skim off any bubbles that occur with a spoon. Add enough hot water to come halfway up the sides of the ramekins. Cover the top of the baking dish with a layer each of baking paper and foil to prevent steam or water getting into the custard. Bake for 35–40 minutes. Check after 35 minutes – the custards are ready when they have a firm jelly-like wobble and the tops are set.

Gently squeeze the bananas while still in their peel to soften the flesh. Set a grill to a medium to high heat and grill until the peel blackens, about 3 minutes on each side. Take off the heat and discard the peel.

To serve, place a ramekin on a serving plate and the banana next to it. Drizzle with extra caramel and coconut cream.

Tapioca Pudding with Mango & Palm Sugar Caramel

Serves 8

2 litres (3½ pt) water
175 g (6 oz) tapioca pearls
250 ml (9 fl oz) Palm Sugar Caramel (see
 page 159)

½ teaspoon sea salt
6 mango cheeks
coconut cream
fresh coconut, shredded

Bring the water to the boil and pour in the tapioca, stirring so that the pearls do not stick to the bottom. Simmer until the pearls become transparent with just a tiny dot of white left in the middle. Pour into a strainer and rinse in cold water.

Place the pearls in a mixing bowl and mix in enough caramel so that the pearls are just swimming. Add the salt.

Cut a mango cheek into slices and place in a serving bowl. Spoon over the tapioca and drizzle with some coconut cream and shredded fresh coconut. Serve.

Tapioca Pudding with Coconut Cream & Vanilla

Serves 8

175 g (6 oz) tapioca pearls
2 litres (3½ pt) water
250 ml (9 fl oz) Sugar Syrup (see page 159)
125 ml (4 fl oz) coconut cream

1½ tablespoons vanilla extract
1½ tablespoons salt
Palm Sugar Ice-cream (see page 142)

Bring the water to the boil and pour in the tapioca, stirring so that the pearls do not stick to the bottom. Simmer until the pearls become transparent with just a tiny dot of white left in the middle. Pour into a strainer and rinse in cold water.

Place the pearls in a mixing bowl and add the rest of the ingredients except the ice-cream. Stir to mix through. Set the mixture in individual 180 ml (6 fl oz) ramekins. Serve with Palm Sugar Ice-cream (see page 142).

Lychee, Coconut Custard & Mango Trifle

A TWIST ON THE TRIFLES SO MANY OF US GREW UP WITH. THE LYCHEES WORK WELL WITH THE CREAMY COCONUT CUSTARD AND THE SMOOTH MANGO JELLY.

SERVES 8

1 x 565 g (18 oz) can lychees, drained
100 ml (3½ fl oz) lychee liqueur
2 mangoes, peeled, stoned and sliced

Mango Jelly
115 g (4 oz) caster (superfine) sugar
125 ml (4 fl oz) water
2 leaves gelatine
1 large mango, peeled, stoned and
    flesh puréed
1½ tablespoons lychee liqueur

Coconut Custard
300 ml (10 fl oz) coconut cream
300 ml (10 fl oz) milk
8 egg yolks
100 g (3½ oz) caster (superfine) sugar

Pandanus Sponge
2 pandanus leaves, finely sliced
3 medium-sized eggs
85 g (2¾ oz) caster (superfine) sugar
1½ tablespoons plain flour
80 g (2⅓ oz) cornflour
1 teaspoon cream of tartar
½ teaspoon bicarbonate of soda
100 ml (3½ fl oz) lychee liqueur

Combine the drained lychees with the liqueur and set aside for about 30 minutes.

TO MAKE THE JELLY, combine the sugar and water in a heavy-based pan and heat gently until the sugar melts. Remove from the heat and add the gelatine. Stir until the gelatine dissolves, then add the mango purée and liqueur. Pour into a shallow container and refrigerate for 1–2 hours until set.

TO MAKE THE COCONUT CUSTARD, combine the coconut cream and milk in a heavy-based saucepan and bring the mixture almost to a boil.

In a separate bowl, whisk the egg yolks and sugar together until thick and pale. While stirring, pour the coconut cream mixture into the egg yolks and whisk together. Return the mixture to the saucepan over a medium heat and stir with a wooden spoon until the mixture coats the back of a wooden spoon. Strain the mixture into a bowl and cool. Refrigerate for at least 1 hour.

TO MAKE THE PANDANUS SPONGE, first make a pandanus essence by blending the leaves with a little water in a blender or food processor. Strain the juice into a small bowl, discarding the solids.

Preheat the oven to 180°C. Grease and line a 25 x 30 cm (10 x 12 in) Swiss roll pan.

Whisk the eggs and sugar until thick and pale. Sift together the flours, cream of tartar and bicarbonate of soda, then gently fold into the egg mixture. Add the pandanus essence and stir though to get an even colour. Pour into the prepared pan and bake for 18–20 minutes until the top is golden and the surface springs back when pressed.

Cool in the pan for 5 minutes before turning out on a wire rack to cool. Drizzle the liqueur over the sponge and set aside. When ready to assemble, cut the sponge into cubes.

To assemble, first place some lychees in the base of a serving bowl. Next, add some sponge and half of the coconut custard. Top with a layer of fresh mango and mango jelly. Repeat, leaving enough room at the top to garnish with fresh mango and lychees.

Mango Pudding with Fresh Shredded Coconut

SERVES 8

4 ripe mangoes, peeled and flesh removed
160 g (5¾ oz) caster (superfine) sugar
5 tablespoons shaved palm sugar
100 ml (3½ fl oz) coconut cream
1 teaspoon sea salt

1 teaspoon pure vanilla extract or
    ½ vanilla bean
flesh of ½ coconut, zested into strips
coconut cream
80 ml (2¾ fl oz) Palm Sugar Caramel (see
    page 159)

Purée the mango and place the purée into a heavy-based saucepan. Turn the heat to a medium level and stir continuously until the mango boils.

Add the sugars, coconut cream, salt and vanilla and continue to cook, stirring constantly until the mixture is thick and a dark yellow brown colour. The mixture is ready when the mango doesn't fall off the spoon when lifted from the mixture. This will take about 20 minutes after the sugars are added.

Oil a small tray and pour the pudding into it and allow to set. Remove the vanilla bean if using.

When cool and set, cut the pudding into 2.5 cm (1 in) squares and roll in the fresh coconut shreds. Place on a serving plate and drizzle with coconut cream and the Palm Sugar Caramel.

Basics

Green Chilli Nahm Jim

Makes 500 ml (18 fl oz)

2 cloves garlic, peeled
3 coriander roots, scraped and cleaned
1 x 3 cm (1¼ in) knob galangal, peeled
60 g (2 oz) palm sugar, crushed
100 ml (3½ fl oz) fish sauce
1 long green chilli, seeded and chopped
4 green bird's eye chillies
300 ml (10 fl oz) lime juice

Pound the garlic, coriander roots, chillies and galangal to a uniform paste in a mortar and pestle. Add the palm sugar and fish sauce, pour over the lime juice and mix thoroughly. The dressing should taste hot, sweet, sour and salty. Add more palm sugar if needed to make it sweeter or fish sauce to make it more salty.

Red Chilli Nahm Jim

Makes about 300 ml (½ pt)

3 red chillies, seeded
2 red bird's eye chillies
2 cloves garlic, peeled
2 coriander roots, scraped and cleaned
1 teaspoon sea salt

60 g (2 oz) palm sugar, shaved
60 ml (2 fl oz) fish sauce
200 ml (7 fl oz) fresh lime juice

Pound the chillies, garlic, coriander roots and salt to a uniform paste in a mortar and pestle.

Add the palm sugar, pound, then add the fish sauce and lime juice. Taste – the flavour should be a balance of sweet, sour and salty.

Chilli Jam

Makes about 250 ml (9 fl oz)

2 litres (3½ pt) vegetable oil
300 g (10½ oz) finely sliced red onions
125 g (4½ oz) garlic, peeled, blended or finely minced
75 g (2¾ oz) dried red chillies, seeded
75 g (2¾ oz) dried prawns (shrimp), soaked in warm water for 10 minutes then drained
1 x 3 cm (1¼ in) piece galangal, peeled, sliced and dry-roasted
100 g (3½ oz) palm sugar, pounded
100 ml (3½ fl oz) fish sauce or 1 tablespoon sea salt
100 ml (3½ fl oz) tamarind pulp

Heat the oil in a wok or a heavy-based saucepan until just smoking.

Fry the onions until they turn the colour of lightly stained pine. Strain through a fine-mesh metal strainer, setting the onions aside to drain. You are using the same oil for each of the fried components of this chilli jam, so you need to strain the oil well.

Fry the garlic until a light golden colour, then remove. Fry the chillies for no more than 10 seconds as they burn quite quickly. Take them out when they are a deep red colour. Place the dried prawns in the oil, moving them around occasionally for about 1 minute. Take out and drain on absorbent paper. Reserve the oil.

Add the galangal to the fried ingredients.

You can make this into a paste in one of several ways:

• pound all the fried ingredients in a large mortar and pestle

SWEET CHILLI SAUCE

MAKES 500 ML (18 FL OZ)

140 g (5 oz) red chillies, seeded
450 g (1 lb) caster (superfine) sugar
250 ml (9 fl oz) cup water
250 ml (9 fl oz) white vinegar
1¹/₂ tablespoons sea salt

Blend the chillies to a paste in a food processor. Set aside.

In a heavy-based saucepan, combine the sugar, water and vinegar. Bring to a gentle boil, add the chillies and salt. Cook for a further 5 minutes, then set aside and cool.

Keep in an airtight container or jar. Use as a dipping sauce or as a dressing with lime juice.

- blend them in a food processor
- use a mincer attachment and mince the ingredients three times and finish by blending in a food processor. This last method gives the best result.

Place the paste in a heavy-based pot, strain the reserved oil over it and stir to combine. Heat the mixture almost to boiling point. When hot, add the palm sugar, fish sauce and tamarind. Stir to mix through, and remove from the heat.

The paste should have a rich, roasted, sweet, sour and salty taste. It is often used as a base to flavour other dishes. Keeps for a few months.

YELLOW BEAN SOY DRESSING

MAKES 750 ML (1 PT 7 FL OZ)

5 cloves garlic, peeled
5 red bird's eye chillies
1 x 4 cm (1¹/₂ in) piece ginger, peeled
250 ml (9 fl oz) light yellow bean soy
250 ml (9 fl oz) thick sweet soy sauce
250 ml (9 fl oz) rice vinegar
125 ml (4 fl oz) thick yellow bean sauce
225 g (8 oz) caster (superfine) sugar

In a mortar and pestle, pound the garlic, chillies and ginger until a uniform paste.

Put the paste and the rest of the ingredients into a heavy-based pot. Bring to the boil and simmer for 5 minutes. Cool and store in a clip-top jar.

CHILLI VINEGAR

A VINEGAR THAT IS ON TABLES IN MOST THAI EATING HOUSES AS AN ACCOMPANIMENT. IT IS USED AS A SIDE DISH TO CUT THE SWEETNESS OF THE CARAMEL AND TO ADD SOME HEAT TO THE RECIPE FOR PORK HOCK (SEE PAGE 122).

MAKES 250 ML (9 FL OZ)

2 large red chillies, finely sliced into rounds
200 ml (7 fl oz) white rice vinegar

Combine the chillies and vinegar and mix well.

Sweet Soy & Ginger Dressing

Makes 500 ml (18 fl oz)

180 ml (6 fl oz) mirin
150 ml (5 fl oz) water
150 ml (5 fl oz) light yellow bean soy
75 ml (2½ fl oz) white vinegar
5 tablespoons caster (superfine) sugar
4 cm (1½ in) knob ginger, peeled and chopped
4 cloves garlic, peeled and finely sliced
3 red bird's eye chillies, sliced into fine rounds
1 teaspoon sesame oil

Bring the mirin, water, yellow bean soy, vinegar and caster sugar to the boil in a heavy-based saucepan over a medium heat. Add the ginger, garlic, chillies and sesame oil. Simmer lightly for 5 minutes, remove from the heat and allow to cool.

Nahm Pla Prik

Makes 125 ml (4 fl oz)

6 red bird's eye chillies, sliced into rounds
1 red shallot, peeled and finely sliced
100 ml (3½ fl oz) fish sauce
juice of ½ lime

Combine all the ingredients and mix well.

Black Bean Sauce

Makes just under 250 ml (9 fl oz)

100 g (3½ oz) salted black beans
200 ml (7 fl oz) vegetable oil
10 cloves garlic, peeled
2 long dried red chillies, seeded
1 x 4 cm (1½ in) knob ginger, peeled
1 tablespoon Chinese black vinegar
2 tablespoons caster (superfine) sugar

Rinse the black beans to remove excess salt and set aside.

Heat the oil in a heavy-based saucepan until just smoking. Blend or pound the garlic to a uniform size (but not a paste) and fry until the colour of lightly stained pine.

Remove the garlic by passing the oil through a wire mesh strainer. Reserve the oil, and place the garlic on absorbent paper to drain.

Pour the hot oil back into the pan, add the chillies and fry for 30 seconds. Remove the chillies and place on absorbent paper. Reserve the oil.

In a food processor, place the black beans, garlic, chillies and ginger and blend to a smooth paste. Add the reserved oil, vinegar and sugar. Pour into a clip-top jar. Keeps indefinitely.

Tamarind

tamarind pulp
warm water

Combine equal amounts of tamarind pulp and warm water and soak for 1–2 minutes to soften. Squeeze to dissolve. Push the paste through a strainer, discarding any seeds and fibres. If the paste is very thick, you may have to dilute with water to taste, especially if you're using in a curry or stir-fry.

Curry Powder

Makes 70 g (2½ oz)

1½ tablespoons coriander seeds
1½ tablespoons fennel seeds
1 teaspoon cumin seeds
1 teaspoon mace
2 dried bird's eye chillies
½ teaspoon ground turmeric
1 teaspoon white pepper

In a bowl combine the coriander, fennel, cumin, mace and chillies. Moisten with cold water and drain immediately. (Wetting the spices helps to cook the spices evenly all the way through without the outside catching and burning.)

Place the wet spice in a wok or heavy-based pan. Roast the spices over a medium heat until fragrant and dry, 5–8 minutes, stirring constantly to ensure they do not burn. Set aside to cool before adding the turmeric and pepper.

When cool, blend the spice mixture in a spice or coffee grinder or pound in a mortar and pestle and sieve through a fine strainer. Store in an air-tight container or a clip-top jar. This mixture keeps for 2–3 weeks before the flavours start to weaken.

GREEN CURRY PASTE

MAKES 375 ML (13 FL OZ)

Paste
1 medium-sized red onion, chopped
5 cloves garlic, peeled
1 x 4 cm (1½ in) piece galangal, peeled
2 stalks lemongrass, white part only
1 teaspoon sea salt
6 coriander roots, scraped and cleaned
6 long green chillies, seeded
8 green bird's eye chillies
2½ tablespoons chopped lesser galangal
1 x 2.5 cm (1 in) piece fresh turmeric
1½ tablespoons roasted shrimp paste
1½ tablespoons grated kaffir lime zest

Spice Mix
1½ tablespoons coriander seeds
1 tablespoon cumin seeds
1 tablespoon mace
1 teaspoon white peppercorns
1 tablespoon sea salt

TO MAKE THE PASTE, pound the onion, garlic, galangal and lemongrass with half the salt in a mortar and pestle until a uniform paste. Remove from the mortar and place in a food processor.

Add to the mortar the coriander roots, chillies, lesser galangal, turmeric, shrimp paste and lime zest. Pound this to a uniform paste, then add to food processor and blend everything to a smooth paste. It should have a good green colour with a hint of fluoro coming from the turmeric.

TO MAKE THE SPICE MIX, wet the coriander, cumin and mace, drain and dry-roast in a small heavy-based pan or wok over a medium heat for

10–15 minutes. This will give all the spices ample time to roast all the way through, and do roast slowly for that length of time as they need to be very fragrant when done. Pound in a mortar and pestle, then grind in small batches in a spice or coffee grinder to a fine powder. Pass through a fine mesh sieve.

Stir the spices into the paste, mix well and place in an airtight container. This paste keeps in a refrigerator for 4–6 days or you can freeze it.

JUNGLE CURRY PASTE

MAKES 250 ML (9 FL OZ)

Paste
1 medium-sized red onion, chopped
5 cloves garlic, peeled
2 stalks lemongrass, white part only
1 x 3 cm (1¼ in) piece turmeric, peeled
6 coriander roots, scraped and cleaned
2½ tablespoons chopped lesser galangal
zest of 1 kaffir lime
1½ tablespoons roasted shrimp paste
6 green chillies, seeded
10 green bird's eye chillies

Spice Mix
2 tablespoons coriander seeds
1 teaspoon cumin seeds
1 teaspoon white peppercorns
1 tablespoon sea salt

TO MAKE THE PASTE, pound the onion, garlic and lemongrass in a mortar and pestle to a uniform paste. Place in a food processor.

Add to the mortar the rest of the ingredients and pound to a uniform paste. Transfer to the food processor and blend everything together to a smooth paste.

TO MAKE THE SPICE MIX, wet the coriander and cumin, drain and dry-roast in a small heavy-based pan or wok over a medium heat for 10 minutes. This will give all the spices ample time to roast all the way through, and do roast slowly for that length of time as they need to be very fragrant when done. Cool, combine with the peppercorns and salt and grind in a spice or coffee grinder to a fine powder. Pass through a fine mesh sieve.

Stir the spices into the paste, mix well and place in an airtight container. This paste keeps in a refrigerator for 4–6 days or you can freeze it.

PEANUT CURRY PASTE

MAKES 250 ML (9 FL OZ)

Paste
1 medium-sized red onion, chopped
5 cloves garlic, peeled
1 x 4 cm (1½ in) piece galangal, peeled
1 stalk lemongrass, white part only, finely sliced
2 tablespoons roasted peanuts
zest of 1 kaffir lime
1 teaspoon roasted shrimp paste
10 long dried chillies, seeded and soaked

Spice Mix
1 tablespoon coriander seeds
1 tablespoon cumin seeds
1 teaspoon white peppercorns
1 tablespoon sea salt

TO MAKE THE PASTE, pound the onion, garlic and galangal in a mortar and pestle to a paste. Place in a food processor.

Add to the mortar the lemongrass, peanuts, lime zest, shrimp paste and chillies and pound to a paste. Add to the food processor and blend to form a smooth red paste.

TO MAKE THE SPICE MIX, wet the coriander and cumin, drain and dry-roast in a small heavy-based pan or wok over a medium heat for 10 minutes. This will give all the spices ample time to roast all the way through, and do roast slowly for that length of time as they need to be very fragrant when done. Cool, combine with the peppercorns and salt and grind in a spice or coffee grinder to a fine powder. Pass through a fine mesh sieve.

Stir the spices into the paste, mix well and place in an airtight container. This paste keeps in a refrigerator for 4–6 days or you can freeze it.

RED CURRY PASTE

MAKES 250 ML (9 FL OZ)

1 medium-sized red onion, chopped
5 cloves garlic, peeled
4 coriander roots, scraped and cleaned
1 x 4 cm (1½ in) piece galangal, finely sliced
1 stalk lemongrass, white part only, finely sliced
1 teaspoon dried prawns (shrimp), soaked in warm water
50 g (1¾ oz) smoked trout
1 tablespoon roasted shrimp paste
10 long dried chillies, seeded and soaked
1 tablespoon sea salt
1 tablespoon white peppercorns, ground

Pound the onion, garlic, coriander roots and galangal in a mortar and pestle until a uniform paste. Place in a food processor.

Pound the remaining ingredients except the peppercorns to a uniform paste and add to the food processor. Blend to a smooth paste. Mix through the pepper.

Store in an airtight container. The paste keeps for 4–6 days in the refrigerator. It freezes well.

RICH RED CURRY PASTE

MAKES ABOUT 250 ML (9 FL OZ)

1 medium-sized onion, peeled and chopped
6 cloves garlic, peeled
1 stalk lemongrass, white part only
1 tablespoon sea salt
1 x 4 cm (1½ in) piece galangal, peeled
6 coriander roots, scraped and cleaned
zest of 2 kaffir limes
8 long dried red chillies, seeded and soaked
1 teaspoon roasted shrimp paste
1½ teaspoons coriander seeds
1 teaspoon white peppercorns

Pound the onion, garlic and lemongrass with the salt in a mortar and pestle to a uniform paste. Place in a food processor.

Pound the galangal, coriander roots and lime

zest and also add to the food processor.

Add to the mortar the chillies and shrimp paste and pound to paste. Transfer to the food processor and blend to a smooth paste. It should smell very fragrant and citrussy.

Wet the coriander, drain and dry-roast in a small heavy-based pan or wok until fragrant. Cool and add the peppercorns and grind in a spice or coffee grinder to a fine powder.

Stir the spices into the paste and seal in an airtight container. This paste keeps for 7 days in the refrigerator or can be frozen.

LIGHT RED CURRY PASTE

MAKES 250 ML (9 FL OZ)

5 cloves garlic, peeled
1 medium-sized red onion, partially dry-roasted
1 stalk lemongrass, white part only, finely sliced
1 x 2.5 cm (1 in) piece galangal, peeled and
    finely sliced
1 tablespoon grated kaffir lime zest
2 coriander roots, scraped and cleaned
4 red bird's eye chillies
1 teaspoon sea salt
1 teaspoon roasted shrimp paste
8 dried red chillies, soaked and seeded
½ teaspoon coriander seeds
½ teaspoon cumin seeds
½ teaspoon white pepper

Pound the garlic, onion, lemongrass, galangal, lime zest, coriander roots and chillies with the salt in a mortar and pestle until a uniform paste. Place in a food processor with the shrimp paste and drained chillies. Blend to a smooth paste.

Wet the coriander and cumin, drain and dry-roast in a small pan or wok until fragrant. Cool and add the peppercorns and grind in a spice or coffee grinder to a fine powder.

Stir the spices into the paste and seal in an airtight container. This paste keeps for 7 days in the refrigerator or can be frozen.

MUSLIM-STYLE CURRY PASTE

MAKES 250 ML (9 FL OZ)

Paste
1 medium-sized red onion, chopped
6 cloves garlic, peeled
1 x 4 cm (1½ in) piece galangal, peeled
1 stalk lemongrass, white part only, finely sliced
6 coriander roots, scraped and cleaned
100 ml (3½ fl oz) water (optional)
10 long red chillies, seeded and soaked

Spice Mix
1½ teaspoon coriander seeds
1 teaspoon cumin seeds
1 cardamom pod
1 x 2.5 cm (1 in) piece cassia bark
3 cloves
½ teaspoon mace
1 star anise
1 tablespoon sea salt

TO MAKE THE PASTE, dry-roast the onion, garlic, galangal, lemongrass and coriander roots in a wok or heavy-based pan until softened, slightly charred and fragrant. If the ingredients are too brown or char too quickly, add the water and cover with a lid on to allow the ingredients to steam and cook all the way through. Remove from the wok when cooked through and cool.

Drain the chillies, combine with the rest of the ingredients and blend to a smooth brownish red paste.

TO MAKE THE SPICE MIX, wet the spices except the salt and dry-roast in a wok or heavy-based pan over a medium heat for 10–15 minutes. This will give all the spices ample time to roast all the way through, and do roast slowly for that length of time as they need to be very fragrant when done. Pound in a mortar and pestle, then grind in small batches in a spice or coffee grinder to a fine powder.

Stir the spices into the paste and add the salt. The paste should be rich and brown in colour and have a heavy spiced smell. Store in an airtight container for up to a week or freeze.

Yellow Curry Paste

Makes 250 ml (9 fl oz)

Paste
1 medium-sized red onion, peeled and chopped
8 cloves garlic, peeled
6 coriander roots, scraped and cleaned
1 x 4 cm (1½ in) piece turmeric, peeled and
    chopped
1 x 4 cm (1½ in) piece ginger, peeled and
    chopped
8 long dried red chillies, seeded and soaked

Spice Mix
1 tablespoon coriander seeds
1 teaspoon cumin seeds
1 teaspoon fennel seeds
½ teaspoon white peppercorns
2 tablespoons sea salt

TO MAKE THE PASTE, place the onion, garlic, coriander roots, turmeric and ginger in a heavy-based pot or wok over a medium heat. Stir until coloured and soft. If the ingredients are taking on too much colour, add a little water to slow down the cooking process. We want the ingredients to caramelise as this is going to give the finished curry depth and added flavour. When the ingredients are soft, scrape into a large bowl and add the drained chillies. Set aside to cool, then blend in a food processor for 3–4 minutes to a smooth reddish yellow paste. If the paste is not wet enough, add a little water to help the move the blades.

TO MAKE THE SPICE MIX, wet the coriander, cumin and fennel, drain and dry-roast in a small heavy-based pan or wok over a medium heat for 5–8 minutes. This will give all the spices ample time to roast all the way through, and do roast slowly for that length of time as they need to be very fragrant when done. Cool, then combine with the peppercorns and salt and grind in small batches in a spice or coffee grinder to a fine powder. Pass through a fine mesh sieve.

Stir the spices into the paste, mix well and place in an airtight container. This paste keeps in a refrigerator for 4–6 days or you can freeze it.

Roasted Rice

Add raw glutinous rice to a dry, heated frying pan. Toast over moderate heat, stirring until the rice is golden brown. Pound until fine in batches using a mortar and pestle or grind in a spice grinder until a fine powder is formed. Store in an airtight container.

Smoking Mix

115 g (4 oz) demarara sugar
200 g (7 oz) glutinous rice
4 kaffir lime leaves
1 piece cassia bark, broken up
2 star anise, broken up
½ cup jasmine tea leaves
1 pandanus leaf, shredded

Combine all the ingredients and mix well.

Salt & Pepper Mix

Makes about 150 g (5 oz)

50 g (1⅔ oz) Sichuan peppercorns
1 teaspoon coriander seeds
1 teaspoon cloves
2 star anise
1 piece cassia bark
5 small dried red chillies
100 g (3½ oz) sea salt

Combine the Sichuan peppercorns, coriander, cloves and star anise in a bowl and cover with water. Drain.

Place the spices in a heavy-based pan and dry-roast over a low heat until the spices have dried out and become fragrant. Add the chillies and continue to dry-roast, stirring constantly for another 2–3 minutes. Remove from the heat and cool.

Add the salt, mix thoroughly and grind in a spice or coffee grinder to a fine powder. Store in an air-tight container.

Roasted Chilli, Sugar & Salt

Something simple to have in the pantry to sprinkle over crisp-fried squid or fried fish with lime juice. Or toss with cashews or peanuts for snacks.

Makes 225 g (8 oz)

200 ml (7 fl oz) vegetable oil
10 dried red chillies, seeded
1 tablespoon sea salt
225 g (8 oz) caster (superfine) sugar

Heat the oil in a saucepan and fry the chillies until they turn a deep red. Remove and dry on absorbent paper.

In a mortar and pestle, place the chillies and salt and pound to a fine powder. Add the sugar and mix through. The mixture should have a deep red tinge to it and a hot, sweet, salty taste.

Pickled Ginger

Early summer is the best time to pickle ginger. When it's young, it's easy to peel and is not too peppery. This is great in salads or as a side dish mixed with cucumber and coriander.

Makes 1 kg (2 lb)

1 kg (2 lb) ginger, peeled and cut into batons
250 ml (9 fl oz) fish sauce
250 ml (9 fl oz) white rice vinegar
225 g (8 oz) caster (superfine) sugar
2 stalks lemongrass, white part only, bruised and sliced
4 kaffir lime leaves
3 red chillies, halved

If using young ginger, wash it and place in a large bowl. If using older ginger, I tend to blanch it 2–3 times in boiling water before proceeding with the recipe.

Place the fish sauce and sugar in a heavy-based pot, bring to the boil and add the lemongrass, lime leaves and chillies. Bring to the boil and pour over the ginger.

Wash the storage jars in hot soapy water. Rinse well in hot water and place on a rack in an oven for 20 minutes on 100°C to sterilise.

Place the hot ginger and pickling liquid in the jar and seal. Leave for 3 weeks before use.

Grilled Aubergine & Chilli Relish

Makes 250 ml (9 fl oz)

4 long green or purple aubergines
6 long red chillies
6 red shallots, unpeeled
6 cloves garlic, unpeeled
1 tomato
1 teaspoon bird's eye chilli powder
50 g (1¾ oz) palm sugar, shaved
50 ml (1¾ fl oz) fish sauce or sea salt
50 ml (1¾ fl oz) tamarind

On a grill plate or in the oven, roast the chillies, aubergines, shallots, garlic and tomato individually until soft and caramelised.

Peel the aubergines – keep the flesh, discard the skin. Peel the shallots, garlic and tomato. Place all the ingredients in a bowl and mix well. Spoon into a mortar and pestle and pound until a uniform rustic relish is achieved. Depending on the size of your mortar, you may need to do this in 2–3 batches.

Flavour with the chilli powder, palm sugar, fish sauce and tamarind. The relish should taste hot, sweet, sour and caramelised.

Eat the relish with fresh cabbage leaves or cucumber, or use as a salad base or as a sauce to accompany grilled meat or fish.

Cucumber Relish

MAKES 500 G (1 LB)

200 ml (7 fl oz) rice vinegar
150 g (5 oz) caster (superfine) sugar
1 piece pickled garlic
2 coriander roots, scraped and cleaned
1 cucumber, diced
1 red shallot, peeled and finely sliced
1 x 2.5 cm (1 in) piece ginger, peeled and
    julienned
1 long red chilli, seeded and julienned
1 small bunch coriander leaves

Boil the vinegar with the sugar, garlic and coriander roots. Strain and cool.

Toss the cucumber, shallot, ginger, chilli and coriander leaves together, then mix into the vinegar mixture. Place in a serving bowl.

Carrot & Daikon Mix

MAKES 500 G (1 LB)

2 medium-sized carrots, peeled and julienned
1 small daikon (mooli), peeled and julienned
sweet vinegar to cover
80 ml (2¾ fl oz) Sweet Chilli Sauce (see page 151)

Mix the carrot and daikon thoroughly in a bowl and pack into a clip-top jar. Pour over enough sweet vinegar to cover, add the sweet chilli sauce and seal. Keeps for 2–3 weeks, refrigerated.

Shrimp Floss

dried shrimp

Place the dried shrimp in a spice grinder and grind until pulverised, about 1 minute.

Spring Onion Pancakes

THESE ARE GREAT FOR PARTIES OR AS A STARTER FILLED WITH ROASTED DUCK FROM CHINATOWN, BEANSPROUTS AND HOISIN SAUCE. OR FILL WITH FINELY CUT BARBECUE PORK AND SERVE WITH CUCUMBER AND CHILLI JAM.

MAKES 25

140 g (5 oz) plain flour
70 g (2½ oz) rice flour
1½ tablespoons sea salt
250 ml (9 fl oz) milk
1 medium-sized egg
70 g (2½ oz) spring (green) onions
    (scallions), finely sliced
1 teaspoon sesame oil
vegetable oil

Combine the flours and salt in a bowl. Make a well in the centre, pour in the milk and whisk until you get a thin, light batter the consistency of pouring cream. Add the egg and stir through the spring onions and sesame oil. Allow to stand in the refrigerator for 30 minutes before cooking.

Heat a non-stick pan to a medium heat and wipe the pan with some vegetable oil.

Using a ladle, pour in just enough batter to cover the base of the pan. Move the pan around so that the mixture coats the base evenly, just like making a crêpe. You want a thin pancake, so it may take a few practice runs.

Cook until the top just sets, then cook the other side. Stack each pancake on a plate and cover with a tea towel as you go. Continue until all the mixture is used up. Do not refrigerate the pancakes if not using immediately – leave them at room temperature.

CRISP-FRIED GARLIC OR SHALLOTS

peeled garlic cloves or shallots
vegetable oil

Slice the garlic or shallots lengthwise. Take care to ensure that all slices are of an even thickness, or they will not cook evenly.

Heat the vegetable oil until just smoking. Test with a piece of garlic or shallot – it should sizzle gently. If it sizzles too furiously and burns almost instantly, the oil is too hot.

Add the garlic or shallots and move them around in the oil to ensure even cooking. When they reach the colour of lightly stained pine, strain through a fine-mesh metal strainer. Toss the garlic or shallots around to remove excess oil and to aerate the chips. Drain on absorbent paper. Store in air-tight container.

PALM SUGAR CARAMEL

MAKES 500 ML (18 FL OZ)

100 ml (3½ fl oz) water
100 g (3½ oz) rock candy, crushed
175 g (6 oz) palm sugar, shaved
85 g (3 oz) black palm sugar, shaved
1 x 3 cm (1¼ in) piece turmeric, peeled
  and sliced
1 pandanus leaf

Combine the water and sugar in a heavy-based pan over a medium heat. Bring to the boil and reduce for 5 minutes. Add the turmeric and pandanus leaf and continue to cook for a further 5 minutes. Take off the heat and allow to cool.

SUGAR SYRUP

MAKES 1.2 LITRES (2 PTS)

500 g (1 lb 2 oz) caster (superfine) sugar
1 litre (1¾ pt) water

Combine the sugar and water in a heavy-based saucepan over a moderate heat and stir until the sugar dissolves.

Glossary

ACIDULATED WATER Water that has lemon or lime juice added to it. Used to prevent fruit and vegetables turning brown once cut.

AUBERGINE, GREEN These look similar to the long purple (Japanese) aubergine. Often served grilled or in stir-fries, curries, salads and relishes. Mild in flavour.

AUBERGINE, PEA Pea-sized dark green berries that grow in small clusters with a bitter flavour. Used in curries and relishes.

AUBERGINE, THAI Round aubergine that may be green, yellow, orange or purple. Used in curries or salads.

BAMBOO SHOOTS Fresh shootscan be found in Chinese or South-East Asian foodshops. The young shoots can differ in size greatly. If using fresh, boil the shoots whole in salted water for 2–3 hours, changing the water twice. When tender, remove and cool. Peel to the creamy centre and cut into batons. Keeps for several days in salted water.

BANANA FLOWER The large purple flower of the banana tree, used in salads and curries. Use a stainless steel knife as other metals discolour the flowers. Discard the outer purple petals until only the inner heart remains. Rub with lemon juice, then quarter the creamy heart lengthwise and remove the core. Finely slice the petals into long strands and keep in acidulated water for 2–3 hours

BANANA LEAF May be deep green or very pale green, depending on the age of the leaves. Available in most Chinese and Thai food stores, where they are sold by weight. They are used to wrap foods such as fish, meat and desserts or for steaming, grilling and baking. The softer, more pliable leaves are best, but if you can only find older leaves,

blanch or steam them for 1–2 minutes before use.

BASIL, HOLY Purple-green leaves with a distinctive pungent, peppery taste, used in stir-fries, jungle curries and dry red curries.

BASIL, THAI A purple-stemmed plant with deep-green, purple-tinged leaves and small flowers. The leaves are used in salads and stir-fries for their fresh, sweet aniseed flavour.

BETEL LEAF Mainly used whole to wrap small morsels and snacks. They have a mild flavour with a little crunch. Torn betel leaves may be added to curries or pickled.

BLACK BEANS Fermented black soybeans popularly used in Chinese cooking. They have a pungent, salty taste and are often used with garlic, and sometimes chilli. Available canned in brine or dried and salted. In this book, I use the dried variety; wash before use to remove the excess salt.

CARDAMOM Used sparingly in some Indian-derived curries. The most readily available are small green pods containing tiny, sticky black seeds with a pungent, camphor-like fragrance. Crush in a mortar and pestle to release their aromatic oils.

CASSIA BARK Related to cinnamon but with larger and coarser quills. It has a stronger flavour than cinnamon. Pound in a mortar and pestle before grinding in a spice grinder.

CHILLIES, BIRD'S EYE The smallest and hottest of the chillies used in Thai cooking, sometimes referred to as 'scuds'. Green chillies have a sharper, fresher flavour and ripen to become red. Dried chillies should not be used in place of fresh ones.

CHILLIES, LONG About 5–10 cm (2–4 inches) long and may be green or red. Green chillies have a sharper, more peppery and herbaceous flavour than the red. In all chillies, the seeds and white membranes contain the most heat, and these may be removed according to taste and heat tolerance.

CHILLIES, LONG, RED DRIED Used in all red curry pastes. To use, snip off the sharp end with a pair of scissors, then run the blade up the side to open up the chilli and scrape away the seeds. Dried chillies may be dry-roasted or rehydrated in warm water.

CHILLI POWDER Made from small red bird's eye chillies. Dry-roast in a frying pan or wok to slightly caramelise, then grind to a powder in a mortar and pestle or spice grinder.

CHINESE CELERY A leafy plant that looks like coriander or flat-leaf parsley with a strong celery-like taste, and available in CFhinese or South-East Asian grocers. Finely sliced celery can be used as a substitute.

CHINESE CHIVES AND FLOWERING CHINESE CHIVES Long, flat-leafed leaves sold in bunches with a distinctive garlic flavour. The flowers may be eaten, too. Widely used in stir-fries or blanched and added to soups and salads.

CLOVES Small, black, woody spices with a distinctive sweet-pungent flavour. Used sparingly in Indian-derived curries and soups.

COCONUT CREAM AND MILK Rich in texture and flavour, both are used extensively in Thai cooking. To make fresh coconut cream and milk, soak finely shredded coconut flesh in hot water, then squeeze through muslin or a tea-towel to extract the milk. Allow the liquid to settle so the cream rises to the top. A fresh coconut will yield around 1 cup coconut cream, regardless of the amount of soaking water used. Also available in cans and tetra-packs, although the flavour is not as good.

COOKING WINE, CHINESE Shaoxing wine is a strong-flavoured Chinese rice wine used in stir-fries and braised dishes. Dry sherry may be substituted at a pinch.

CORIANDER Also known as cilantro, it is used extensively in Thai cooking for its unique spicy flavour. Select dark, green lush bunches with roots still attached. The roots are used to make Thai curry pastes.

CORIANDER, FLAT-LEAF A long-leafed variety of coriander that grows in clusters with spiky-edged leaves. It tastes slightly stronger than coriander and is shredded into salads and hot and sour soups.

CORIANDER SEEDS Small, light brown seeds of the coriander plant that have a clean, fragrant citrus flavour that is enhanced when roasted.

CUMIN An essential component of many Asian spice blends, these tiny brown seeds have a strong, earthy, fennel-like flavour.

DRIED SHRIMP These add a unique, pungent, salty taste to stir-fries, salads and curry pastes. Select ones with an intense bright orange colour.

FENNEL SEEDS Small, greenish seeds with an intense liquorice flavour used in many Indian-style pickles, chutneys and breads.

FERMENTED BEANCURD Made by fermenting slightly dried, small cubes of bean-curd with a red rice mould. Fermented beancurd may be flavoured with chilli, sesame oil or wine. May be eaten on its own or used (sparingly) in stir-fries, where it breaks down into the sauce to add a thick, creamy texture.

FISH SAUCE Considered the salt of Thailand, fish sauce is used in many savoury dishes to add depth and character. It is made from small fermented fish such as anchovies. The clear brown liquid is bottled and most brands contain salt and fish juice. On its own fish sauce is rather pungent, and it is usually mixed with lime juice and palm sugar, where its saltiness is balanced with the sour and sweet flavours.

GALANGAL A rhizome from the same family as ginger and turmeric. It has a peppery, almost iodine-like aroma and is used in curry pastes and soups. Use young shoots if possible.

GARLIC, PICKLED Young garlic, pickled in a vinegary brine and sold in jars. It is used in curries and chopped into noodle dishes, salads and stir-fries.

GINGER A must in any kitchen, its sweet peppery taste lending itself well to Thai or other Asian dishes. Young rhizomes are pinkish-white, with a translucent skin. These are preferred in Thai cooking as they have a milder flavour. Avoid ginger that is wrinkled and dry.

HOISIN SAUCE A thick, sweet and fragrant sauce made from fermented soybeans, flavoured with garlic, sesame and five-spice or star anise. It is mainly used in Chinese cooking with duck and pork.

KAFFIR LIME AND ZEST A round, knobbly, deep green citrus fruit, mainly used for its zest in curry pastes. The juice is very intense, and a little is sometimes added to fresh lime juice for use in dressings.

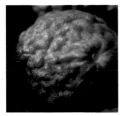

KAFFIR LIME LEAF Dark glossy double-leaves with an aromatic citrus flavour, used to flavour curries and soups and may be finely shredded and mixed through salads. Fresh leaves are preferable, but frozen leaves will do in pastes and marinades.

LEMONGRASS A tall, lemon-scented stalk used extensively in Thai cooking. The tender, pale bottom part is finely sliced and used in curry pastes and salads. Scraps can be bruised and used to add flavour to soups and braises.

LESSER GALANGAL (KRACHAI) I call it 'wild' ginger as there is no real translation for this rhizome. It sits in the same family as ginger and galangal and is sometimes known as Chinese keys. Lesser galangal has an earthy, peppery flavour and is essential in jungle curries. It grows in finger-like clumps, and is sometimes available fresh from Asian grocers. It can also be purchased pickled in brine.

LIME Fresh lime juice is an essential ingredient in Thai cooking, and added to all kinds of dishes for a vibrant piquancy. Lime juice is also combined with fish sauce and palm sugar to make salad dressings.

LIMES, PICKLED Popular in Thai cooking, and may be sweet or salty. Used whole in some soups and steamed dishes, and are available from Asian food stores.

LONGAN A similar fruit to a lychee, longans grow in clusters. The fruit has a brown skin and sweet, crunchy, juicy flesh.

LOTUS ROOT A rhizome that looks like two or three sausages joined together! It is a starchy white root with a crisp texture that is retained when cooked. Lotus roots have a slightly sweet and nutty flavour. Peel and wash before use and cut into 10 mm (½ in) discs.

LYCHEE A summer fruit, and most varieties have a hard outer skin and a soft, moist, deliciously perfumed, white flesh and a large seed.

MACE The outer casing around the nutmeg with a similar taste but not as strong. Often used in curry pastes.

MORTAR AND PESTLE Essential for grinding fibrous roots, herbs and spices and to make wet and dry pastes and spice mixes. They come in all shapes and sizes, made from granite, stone and clay. If you have the time and patience to use one, the result will always be superior.

MUSTARD GREENS, PICKLED A member of the cabbage family, mustard greens come pickled in a salty brine and vacuum packed. Rinse well before use. At Longrain we then store them in a home-made brine, made by bringing equal amounts of sugar and white wine vinegar to the boil and infusing with chilli, kaffir lime leaf and lemongrass. The mustard greens are added to the brine, returned to the boil and then transferred to an air-tight container. Pickled mustard greens make a delicious side dish and are also good added to stir-fried dishes.

OIL, SESAME Strongly flavoured oil made from sesame seeds that is widely used in Chinese cookery, but should be used sparingly as too much can taste bitter. Best diluted with vegetable oil to make it less overpowering. It also burns very easily.

PALM SUGAR A hard dense sugar made from the sap of the sugar palm tree, boiled down and set into discs. Palm sugar has a sweet almost treacle-like flavour. Many varieties are available from Asian grocers – Thai, Indonesian (gula jawa), Malaysian (gula melaka). Unless specified, for the dishes in this book I use golden Thai palm sugar.

PANDANUS LEAF Also known as 'screwpine' leaves, these dark green leaves come from the pandanus palm. They are used for their wonderful fresh grassy flavour and their vibrant green colour in desserts, but may also be used to perfume boiled rice and curries. Whole leaves may be used to wrap food.

PAPAYA, GREEN The flesh of the green papaya can be shredded finely and soaked in iced water to give it a good crunch. Or cut into bite-sized pieces and added to soups and yellow curries.

PEPPERCORNS, SICHUAN The dried berry of the prickly ash tree, not related to ordinary peppercorns. They have a tingly, fiery, peppery flavour.

PEPPERCORNS, WHITE Used as a dried spice ingredient in many curry pastes and braises. More commonly used than black pepper in Thai cookery.

POMELO A large, yellow-skinned citrus fruit, similar to a grapefruit, pomelos have either yellow or pink flesh. Not as bitter as grapefruit and can be used in salads or desserts. Peel as you would grapefruit; the large segments break away easily. Discard all the white pith and use only the flesh.

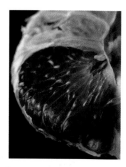

RICE FLOUR Made from finely ground, long-grain rice, rice flour is mainly used to make desserts, wonton wrappers and noodles.

ROCK CANDY Large chunks of sugar that must be pounded in a mortar and pestle before use. It is a very pure sugar that dissolves to make a clear syrup. It adds a nice shine to sauces, braises and soups.

SHALLOTS Small reddish onions used in curries and braised dishes. They are often fried for use as a crisp garnish for salads, curries and grilled dishes. When making curries, you can substitute with purple or Spanish onions.

SHRIMP PASTE A 'signature' flavour in Thai cooking, shrimp paste is added to all kinds of curry pastes, dressings and relishes. Fermented shrimp paste is a dense, brown, pungent paste that may be used raw or slightly roasted to mellow its intensely fishy flavour. Traditionally, it is wrapped in banana leaves and grilled over the embers of a fire. In Western kitchens, a similar result can be achieved by wrapping it in aluminium foil and dry-frying in a heavy pan or roasting in the oven.

SOY SAUCE The brand of soy we use at Longrain – 'Healthy Boy Formula 1' – is made from fermented yellow beans and is a lighter-style sauce. Soy sauce can be used as a substitute for fish sauce in recipes if you are a vegetarian.

SOY SAUCE, THICK SWEET Sweet Indonesian soy sauce also known as ketjap (or ketcap) manis is a thick soy sauce made from fermented soybeans and brewed with palm sugar or molasses. I recommend the 'ABC' brand, which is from Indonesia.

SPRING (GREEN) ONION Also known as scallions, these long, green and white onions are used in salads, stir-fries and sauces.

TAMARIND Extracted from the pods of tamarind trees and compressed into dark-brown sticky blocks, tamarind is used as a souring agent in soups, salads, stir-fries and curries.

TAPIOCA, PEARLS Small transparent balls made from tapioca flour. Used as a thickener in some Thai dishes and as a dessert, where it is often flavoured with sugar syrup and coconut cream. Do not rinse under water, or they will clump together to form a soggy mass.

TAPIOCA STARCH Flour made from the starch of the cassava root, used in desserts, batters and as a thickening agent.

TURMERIC A rhizome related to the ginger family, probably best known for its distinct yellow gold colour and distinctive earthy flavour. Turmeric is available fresh and dried, but are not interchangeable. Fresh turmeric is most commonly used as a vegetable. Dried turmeric is used in curry powders.

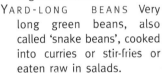

VINEGAR, BLACK Vinegar made from glutinous rice and water, and aged for 10 years, used to give depth to braised dishes, stir-fries and soups. I recommend the brand 'Chen Kiang'.

VINEGAR, RICE A clear 'white' vinegar similar to regular white vinegar. Rice vinegar has a subtler taste and is not as strong as the Western white version. It is used in side dishes and stir-fries.

VINEGAR, SWEET Equal parts of white vinegar and sugar are mixed with coriander root and pickled garlic, brought to the boil and simmered until the sugar melts. Sweet vinegar is used in salad dressings and in side dishes.

WATER CHESTNUTS The corm of a type of underwater grass. Fresh water chestnuts are available at the end of winter and beginning of spring. They add a delicious crunch to stir-fries, and can be cut finely and used in fillings for spring rolls and dumplings.

WINGBEANS An unusual-looking bean with four distinctive ridges running along their sides. Wingbeans range in colour from light to dark green. Top and tail as for normal beans. They may be eaten blanched or raw with relishes or added to salads, stir-fries or vegetable curries.

YARD-LONG BEANS Very long green beans, also called 'snake beans', cooked into curries or stir-fries or eaten raw in salads.

YELLOW BEAN SOY, LIGHT Made from fermented yellow soy beans, this is the main soy sauce I use for the recipes in this book.

YELLOW BEAN PASTE, THICK A paste-like sauce with the actual beans in it. I use this sauce in stir fries or blend it to a smooth paste and add it to caramelised palm sugar to make dressings. I recommend the 'Healthy Boy Formula 1' brand.

Index

Acknowledgements

Grateful thanks to all of Longrain's loyal customers.

Thanks to Longrain's 'book' team: Sam, Jeremy, Mark, Foong Ling and Lindy Loo.

Thanks to the Longrain 'fathers' – John Sample and Leo Christie and Ros Sample, Justin, Jackie and Alicia. To all of Longrain's kitchen, restaurant and bar staff, and our long-term staff members – Lynley, Lewie, Fong, Zowie and Kitsana – thank you.

Thanks to my Mum and Ian, Oma and Opa.

Thanks to Longrain's long-term suppliers: Murdoch Produce, Demcos, Utopia Foods, Nicholas Foods, Pontip and Hong Lee. Thanks to Kasumi Knives.

Thanks to my fellow mentors and chefs: David Thompson, Alex Herbert, David King and Andrew Mirosch.

Sam would like to thank Nikki, his Mum Ann, Clive Smith and Jeremy Shipley.

Lindy would like to thank Vicki Wild for her guidance.

The authors and publishers are grateful to Hanimex's Jacques Guerinet and Deidre McAlinden for supplying us with Fujifilm Professional.

Thanks to Sam Robinson for her 'Longrain' range of handmade pottery, designed by Samsar Designs (samsardesigns@bigpond.com).

Thanks to Garrett Robinson for his fishy shot.

Thanks also to Sydney College of the Arts' Ceramic Department and Pioneer Studios.

Thanks to Rose Porteous.